Finding the Way

Finding the Way

Restarting Your Journey with Jesus

Bruce McNab

WIPF & STOCK · Eugene, Oregon

FINDING THE WAY
Restarting Your Journey with Jesus

Copyright © 2013 Bruce McNab. All rights reserved. Except for brief quotations in critical publications or reviews, no part of this book may be reproduced in any manner without prior written permission from the publisher. Write: Permissions, Wipf and Stock Publishers, 199 W. 8th Ave., Suite 3, Eugene, OR 97401.

Wipf & Stock
An Imprint of Wipf and Stock Publishers
199 W. 8th Ave., Suite 3
Eugene, OR 97401
www.wipfandstock.com

ISBN 13: 978-1-62032-826-2

Manufactured in the U.S.A.

All rights reserved. No part of this publication may be reproduced, stored in a retrieval system, or transmitted in any form or by any means—electronic, mechanical, photocopy, recording, or any other—except for brief quotations in printed reviews—without the permission of the author, except as provided by United States of America copyright law.

All Scripture quotations (except from the Psalms), unless otherwise indicated, are from the Revised Standard Version of the Bible, copyright © 1952 [2nd edition, 1971] by the Division of Christian Education of the National Council of the Churches of Christ in the United States of America. Used by permission. All rights reserved.

Scripture quotations marked NRSV are from the New Revised Standard Version Bible, copyright © 1989 by the Division of Christian Education of the National Council of the Churches of Christ in the USA. Used by permission. All rights reserved.

Scripture passages taken from The Message, copyright © 1993, 1994, 1995, 1996, 2000, 2001, 2002, used by permission of NavPress Publishing Group.

All quotations from the Psalms are from the Psalter of The Book of Common Prayer, copyright © 1986 by The Church Pension Fund. All rights reserved.

This book is dedicated to Joan,
my wife, best friend, and ministry partner.
Without her encouragement and patient help
I could never have written it.

*Jesus said,
"I am the way,
and the truth,
and the life.
No one comes to the Father
except through me."*

—THE GOSPEL ACCORDING TO JOHN 14:6

*Without the Way, there is no going,
Without the Truth, there is no knowing.
Without the Life, there is no living.*

—THOMAS À KEMPIS, *THE IMITATION OF CHRIST*

Contents

Acknowledgments ix
Preface xi

Prologue: The Disciples' Journey 1

1. Deciding to Follow Jesus 7
2. Discovering the Bible 24
3. Experiencing God's Love 37
4. Responding to God's Love: Worship 53
5. Responding to God's Love: Prayer 67
6. Responding to God's Love: Loving Your Neighbor as Yourself 89
7. Living with a Purpose 103
8. Finding a Church 119
9. Putting It All Together: Christianity as a Way of Life 139

Epilogue: Jesus Is Looking for Disciples, Not Admirers 153
Appendix A. Bibles and Bible Reading 159
Appendix B. Recommended Books 165
Bibliography 169

Acknowledgments

I AM GRATEFUL FOR the encouragement I received from William H. Willimon at the beginning of this project. Will was the person who first suggested the idea that I reach out personally to younger adults and help them discover how to reengage in a meaningful way with their faith and with the church. He read the rough draft of my first few chapters and encouraged me to persevere. My spiritual mentor, longtime bishop, and friend, Bill Frey, read the manuscript at an early stage and gave the effort his blessing, which was a tremendous boost to me.

I'm thankful for the diligent work of my old friend and former colleague in ministry, Geoff Gwynne, who served virtually as an unpaid editor—reading and rereading the manuscript, correcting errors large and small, challenging my thinking, asking good theological questions, and gently but wisely recommending various strategic revisions. I was also blessed by good advice from my friends Peter Grenney, Dave Hatfield, Rob Johnson, Paul Kurkulis, Greg Powell, Mary Kate Réjouis, and Chris Tolk, all of whom read portions of the manuscript at different stages and offered helpful suggestions.

Most importantly, I am indebted to my wife and ministry partner, Joan, who carefully read every version of every chapter, correcting errors each time, and giving me constant love and encouragement during the time it took to research and write *Finding the Way*.

Preface

ONE OF THE MOST fulfilling experiences of my last year in parish ministry before retirement was to be mentor and friend to a monthly gathering of younger adults—some single, but most married, and many with small children. Most of them were raised in a church, but dropped out in high school or college and, except for perhaps being married in the church, did not participate in a worshiping community for a number of years. The times we spent together talking freely made me aware of the earnestness with which some men and women in their thirties and early forties, busy and often distracted by careers and parenting, want to find a way to make the journey of life guided by Jesus, with God at the center of their lives and the lives of their families.

These seekers want to return to meaningful religious practice or—more often—find it for the first time. I'm writing this book for them. But I'm also writing for people who have never dropped out of church, who might be middle-aged or even older, but who recognize they need a fresh start on their spiritual journey—a new way of looking at Jesus and understanding how to follow him in the twenty-first-century world. Both groups—"returnees" and "restarts"—are undergoing a kind of conversion. This isn't a matter of turning to another religion, but of turning to Jesus in a new way. This conversion experience is a process for them, not a one-time, dramatic, "out of the darkness into the light" transformational moment.

I'm writing for people who, by returning to the church after a long season away—or maybe simply by reading this book—are manifesting at least a tentative desire to know Christ and discover new meaning and fresh purpose for their lives by following him. What I have to say here is for people who have already decided Jesus deserves serious attention, and who want to make a break with their old life and embrace a new way of living that will lead them to a new kind of thinking. I'm writing for men and women who want to turn to Jesus and center their lives in the God whom

Jesus reveals. I'm not addressing people who are content with simply being churchgoers. That's why this book is entitled *Finding the Way*. I want to give practical help to people who are hungry for a personal relationship with God and a living faith they can understand clearly, explain simply, practice faithfully, and share with their children and friends.

In the following chapters, I offer ideas about the Christian way, organized with my target audience of returnees and restarts in mind. I begin with the simple decision to follow Jesus and continue with discovering one's place in the great story of the Bible, experiencing God's love, responding to God's love with worship, prayer, and love for our neighbors, discerning a higher purpose for life, finding a church community, and then putting all these things together as an identifiably Christian way of living, tolerating life's inevitable ambiguities and uncertainties and determining to trust the providence of God. *Finding the Way* will be most useful to those who read its chapters in numerical order rather than skipping around, since each new chapter presumes familiarity with all the earlier ones. At the end of each chapter is a short section of bullet points offering ways readers might implement some of the ideas in that chapter. Finally, there are two appendixes in the back of the book, one to help those who are interested in starting to read the Bible daily, and the other listing some books that I recommend to anyone serious about practicing Christianity as a way of life.

I write from a limited cultural context. I'm a white, middle-class American who has spent forty years in the ordained ministry of the Episcopal Church. I love my church, but I know it's not the only way to live a life of faithfulness to Christ. Each of us who chooses to journey with Jesus must find the right way for ourselves, but we will always make that journey as members of a community of fellow travelers. If we search, we'll find the community that fits us best.

No stunning insights will be disclosed in these pages. I'm a priest and pastor, not a professional theologian, and this book is mainly a personal testament of faith. My goal is pastoral: to offer serious seekers a convenient, practical synthesis of ideas originally articulated by more eloquent, holy, and visionary people than I am—ideas that I hope will supply direction and inspiration for a renewed, Christ-centered way of life for women and men who are living, working, and raising families in America today.

I would have nothing at all to write if I had not been helped in countless ways by the probing questions, humble confessions, touching experiences, and Spirit-filled revelations that have been shared with me by the saints who have been my friends over the last four decades, and especially the young adults I am thinking about as I write this book. Their hunger for God inspires me.

Bruce McNab
Bozeman, Montana
October 26, 2012

Prologue: The Disciples' Journey

LIFE IS A LONG and complex journey for everybody, and each of us must find our own way forward. Christians are people who have decided to make the journey of life with Jesus Christ as their Guide.[1] The metaphor of the journey occurs in the literature of many religions, obviously because it's so apt. Everyone who writes about religious experience tries to describe what the path is like, the long road that is the soul's way home to God, in hope of helping fellow travelers along at least the portions of that road we've already traversed, mindful that we ourselves still have a long way to go.

I don't exaggerate my competence in this regard. I'm a Christian because of a spiritual formation that began in childhood, and I'm an ordinary pastor. But I trust that I might aid others by identifying some of the common stages on the Christian journey, as well as a few of the confusing side trails and places where the path is almost hidden by the weeds that inevitably grow up around it.

For me, religion is good, though it's often misunderstood, which is why there are so many people these days who claim to be "spiritual but not religious." The Latin root of the word *religion* comes from a combination of *re* ("again") plus *ligare* ("to bind")—giving it the essential meaning of "to reconnect." At least this is what Augustine thought at the end of the fourth century, and we're wise to accept his understanding of the etymology, since he was a formally-trained Latin rhetorician. "Religion," using Augustine's understanding, *reconnects* human beings with God, who is our common Source and common final End, but from whom we are now separated. But religion that is ritual alone, sacrament alone, cannot satisfy the restlessness, the instability, that Augustine famously observed is present in human hearts that have not found their stability in God.[2] True religion entails *per-*

---

1. I realize the New Testament never calls Jesus by the title "Guide," but since Jesus told his disciples, "Follow me," it seems self-evident that he intended to be their guide. Therefore, I see the title as rooted in the gospels, even though it is not explicitly used there.

2. Augustine's Latin phrase, commonly rendered literally, "you have made us for

sonal engagement with the mysterious but loving Thou who is addressing us not only through Scripture and liturgy, but from our own inner depths. Michael Casey, an Australian Cistercian writer and theologian, makes the point better than I when he writes,

> There are many church-going persons who exclude themselves from a more intense encounter with the divine otherness, and do not allow their religion to influence their behavior. In such cases, it eventually becomes evident that *outward observance, however holy, cannot take the place of personal encounter with the living God*. Rituals are no more than lifeless superstitions unless something is happening at the deep center of personal being. It is this dark intrapersonal bonding with the Unseen that is the basis of genuine religion, and the spark by which our spiritual faculties are activated. Christians call this mysterious reality "faith." It is gift, and not achievement; nor is it merely a cognitive event; we perceive that it is the work of God deep in our souls.[3]

My goal is to inspire readers to make themselves progressively more available to God through obedience to Christ and, in so doing, to discover that Christianity is a way of life, not merely a set of doctrines.

I don't presume to have all the answers. In fact, as I get older I'm not sure I even understand all the questions. I do not imagine there's one size that fits all, and I present my ideas with the prayer that some of them may contribute to readers' growth in love for God. I have no interest in polemics. I'm not writing to score debating points, defend "orthodoxy," or change the minds of those who doubt that we finite creatures are able to grasp any of the purposes of the infinite God. I benefitted from reading Karen Armstrong's book *The Case for God*.[4] Armstrong, like Christian thinkers both eastern and western from the patristic era to the Protestant Reformation, argues that those who profess faith nevertheless cannot presume to define the attributes of God beyond the Divine's transcendence and ineffability. We can only safely say what we are sure the Deity is not. This *via negativa* approach to Christian spirituality understands that God is "no thing," neither an entity nor an object among other objects in the universe upon which we

---

yourself, and our hearts are restless till they find their rest in you" (*quia fecisti nos ad te et inquietum est cor nostrum donec requiescat in te*), is paraphrased in this way by Garry Wills in his fresh translation of the *Confessions*: "you made us tilted towards you, and our heart is unstable until stabilized in you." Augustine, *Confessions*, 3.

3. Casey, *Fully Human*, 204 (italics added).
4. See especially pp. 6, 124–26, 281–82.

might focus the tools of human inquiry. Consequently, we cannot name God as "the Supreme Being," because doing so makes God merely a part of the furniture of the universe. God is author of the universe, not a being within it—not even its *supreme* being. God is as separate and distinct from his creation as Michelangelo was separate from his Sistine Chapel frescoes.

God is wholly other, beyond the reach of even the greatest human minds. "Left to ourselves," Armstrong says, "we could know nothing at all about God." [5] Nevertheless, we who are people of faith put our trust in God for reasons, including experiential reasons, that are persuasive to us, though our reasons are not the kind that can be subjected to the empirical analysis that might be applied, for instance, to the reasons a planetary scientist offers for believing that water flows beneath the arid landscape of Mars.

The hidden God is not available to our unaided intellect.[6] We can only know God, or even know *about* God, because of God's self-manifestation, God's immanence. Christianity is and always has been a religion of revelation. And God's self-revelation demands that human beings *experience* that revelation in a meaningful way, even if our experiences are secondhand. I believe we finite creatures *can* grasp some of the purposes of the infinite God, especially to the extent that God's purposes deal with us. However, we must always take care, as Alan Jones warns in *Journey into Christ*, not "to bully and coerce others with our experiences."[7] People like Karen Armstrong are rightly suspicious of those who presume to generalize about their private experiences of God.

The Bible is the documentary testimony to divine revelation most readily accessible to those likely to read this book. It is through reflection on the sacred Scriptures and the collective religious experience of the church, as well as my own experiences of sixty-odd years on the journey, that I arrive at the observations and opinions in this book. I say the Bible is the record of God's revelation, but I don't believe revelation itself has ever been exclusively about mere language—nouns, verbs and modifiers, independent and subordinate clauses, and the like. "It is possible for any literate person to read the Bible; to find in its pages words of eternal life is

5. Ibid., 105.
6. See Allen, *Theology*, 1–14. Allen provides a clear exposition of God's transcendence and immanence.
7. Jones, *Journey*, 58.

something that flesh and blood cannot reveal."[8] That revelation is a work of the Holy Spirit, and minus the operation of the Spirit, the bare text of the Bible remains, as one of my mentors once called it, "double-columned boredom."

God's self-disclosure is best described by the Fourth Evangelist, who writes: "the *Logos* became flesh and lived among us" (John 1:14, italics added). Christians believe this matter of the Word becoming flesh applies particularly to the incarnation of God in Christ, but we might also think of it as happening through the multiple ways God has revealed himself by interaction with us, his human children, and through the continuing inspiration of his Spirit in those who turn their hearts to him and choose the perspective of faith. Kenneth Leech writes, "The reality of God is a continually experienced reality, the God not of the philosophers but of Abraham, Isaac and Jacob, and of many thousands since their day. *The God of biblical faith is a God who is known only in the context of a shared and lived experience.* Without that experience, God remains an intellectual abstraction."[9]

A legitimate debate has been under way since the first Christian century about whether or to what extent we encounter God in the historical person of Jesus of Nazareth. I don't intend to engage in that debate. I am a Christian, and I write from the conviction that Jesus Christ discloses the essential truth of the eternal God that we need in order to have a relationship with God—not *all* the truth, since God is more than anyone can ever imagine and his fullness is beyond our capacity to experience or describe, but nevertheless *sufficient* truth to inspire us to trust Jesus as our guide and pattern for living.[10]

In America and western Europe the institutional church is in decline, particularly among post-Boomer generations. Church leaders want to respond to this situation, and religious writers churn out scores of books on the subject every year. Some look for the solution in a return to more

---

8. Casey, *Fully Human*, 201.

9. Leech, *Experiencing God*, 25–26 (italics added).

10. I find it tedious to write about God without ever using any pronouns. I will follow the conventional and traditional English language practice of referring to the Deity with masculine rather than feminine (or neuter) pronouns, trusting readers to understand that I do not regard God as essentially (or even mainly) "like" a male person, even when I write of God as "Father," following the usage of Jesus.

traditional liturgical observances, doctrinal purity, and strictly enforced moral discipline. Others think radical institutional restructuring, wider inclusivity, and a de-emphasis on dogma will make the difference. My sympathies lie with those who believe the church needs to reform its structures and rethink its customs. But my deepest conviction is that what the church needs most of all—both from lambs who had wandered away from the flock but are now coming back, and from old sheep who may have strayed a bit, but never very far—is renewed personal devotion to the journey with Jesus, rededication to the imitation of Christ.

I admire the way Michael Casey describes the New Testament portrayal of Jesus' mission:

> Throughout the Gospels there are two salient aspects of the identity of Jesus. He is from the Father, sent by God to accomplish a task. Secondly, the human journey of Jesus is one that leads back toward God. It is this movement back toward God that is opened to believers of all generations. In following Jesus, we are shown the way that leads toward the Father. Our life is not aimless; it has a destination. We have not been left to wander in the desert; the Shepherd has come to seek what is lost and bring us home.[11]

---

11. Casey, *Toward God*, 2.

Chapter 1

Deciding to Follow Jesus

After this many of his disciples drew back and no longer went about with him. Jesus said to the twelve, "Do you also wish to go away?" Simon Peter answered him, "Lord, to whom shall we go? You have the words of eternal life; and we have believed, and have come to know, that you are the Holy One of God."

—JOHN 6:66–69

YOUNG ADULTS RETURNING TO church after years of absence are looking for a religious experience that feels personally relevant and more spiritually vital than what they recall from the church of their childhood, and older people who want to restart their spiritual journey no longer care to participate in the same old ecclesiastical "business as usual." Returnees and restarts alike are attracted to the person of Jesus, but their confirmation classes (if they had any) were twenty years ago or more, and they've had no significant experience of Christian formation since. They are eager to learn, hungry for inspiration, looking for spiritual community, and hoping to begin experiencing Christianity as a way of life for themselves and their children, rather than merely as a formal belief system to which they are asked to give intellectual assent. Both groups want a deeper, more personal and less dogmatic meaning to their identity as Christians, but neither have much interest in the institutional church.

If returnees and restarts choose to follow Jesus afresh as their guide on life's journey, what shape will that new way of life take—especially for young adults absorbed by the daily preoccupations typical of their generation? What specific practices are likely to help neophyte disciples stick with their

Finding the Way

guide and not be deterred by the inevitable frustrations and distractions that will arise to hinder their progress on the trail? To borrow a metaphor from rock climbing, about which I have learned a little from our two teenage Montana grandsons: Are there secure finger- and toe-holds I might, from personal experience, point out to those who are starting up this steep rock face which is the way that leads to Life?

I'm aware that the younger adults I see returning to church are only a small fraction of the total number that drifted away. Many people in America raised in a church have abandoned it completely and show little interest in coming back. Church membership and attendance is in slow decline, even though a Gallup Poll taken in May 2011 showed that more than nine out of ten still say yes when asked the basic question, Do you believe in God? (That ratio is down only slightly from 1944, the dark days of World War II.)[1] It's important to recognize that abandonment of a church denomination is *not* the same thing as rejection of Jesus Christ, although it does mean rejection of, or at least disillusionment with, "organized Christianity"—that is, the institutional church. A 2009 survey by the Pew Forum on Religion and Public Life found that

> Rather than leaving religion over a loss of belief, most of the formerly religious were responding to what it calls "disenchantment with people and institutions." For instance, more than half of Americans who were raised Roman Catholic or Protestant but have left the faith say that religious people are judgmental, hypocritical, or insincere and cite that as a major reason for leaving. Among that same group, almost half complain that religious organizations focus on rules at the expense of spirituality. And roughly 40 percent of unaffiliated former Catholics and Protestants said their spiritual needs weren't being met. The fact that so many of the religiously unaffiliated say they have spiritual needs makes it difficult to see them as poster children for a booming secular class. Indeed, the Pew survey finds that only a third of former Catholics and Protestants who are now unaffiliated say that modern science proves that religion is superstition. Roughly 4 in 10 of the unaffiliated, meanwhile, say that religion is still at least somewhat important to their lives. *And roughly a third of those who were raised*

---

1. Newport, "More," n.p.

Catholic or Protestant but are now unaffiliated say they have just not found the right religion yet.[2]

My unscientific assessment is that there are countless younger church returnees and older restarts who want to experience a fresh religious encounter, have a spiritual center for their daily lives, and possess a faith they can embrace and share. But many who are attracted to Jesus and interested in the Christian way also feel hindered by aspects of their daily lives. These hindrances range from vocational and economic distractions (just making a living and paying the bills is a huge task) to the legitimate demands of child-rearing (children consume a lot of their time and energy), negative fixations with entertainment or personal appearance (everybody wants to have some fun, and looking good often makes us feel good), and a fundamental lack of self-discipline (few of us are taught how to say no to our appetites or ambitions). As children, most were not taught the Bible, with its themes of creation, sin, judgment, repentance, regeneration, and new life. Certainly they were not taught it the way my Bible-soaked generation was, back in the middle of the last century. And no one has yet given them the pastoral nurture, inspiration, or encouragement that helps in surmounting these obstacles.

The essential first step for an earnest returnee or restart, a "wannabe" disciple of Jesus, is a personal statement of commitment (or recommitment) to follow Jesus in the journey of life. I'm not referring to a church event like a confirmation service, but rather a quiet, simple declaration in the presence of at least one other person, such as a pastor or Christian friend. This needs to be an unpressured, voluntary act, witnessed by someone else. Such an initial commitment need not include affirmation of a creed or any other formal statement of doctrine. For the sake of integrity, any theological declaration more complex than "I have decided to follow Jesus" probably should wait for later. I don't say this because I think that what we understand about God or how we describe the person and work of Christ is unimportant; on the contrary, I think they are vitally significant. But newly committed disciples should spend time following Jesus on the journey and reflecting on that experience, reading Scripture, worshiping with the church, praying alone and with friends, and allowing the Spirit of God to work in their lives *before* putting their beliefs into an intellectual, propositional form, either using their own words or one of the historic creeds of the church.

2. Gilgoff, "Many Americans," n.p. (italics added).

Finding the Way

People can make a commitment to follow Jesus even when they're still struggling with distractions and obstacles of the sort I listed above. A friend of mine who's a forty-something husband and father of two describes his personal history of frustrations and challenges this way: a parent dying of cancer, loss of several jobs, the time squeeze that goes with working and raising kids, marriage problems, debt issues, the struggle to feel personal worth in the face of painful defeats, wonder about life's larger meaning and purpose, frustration that he might never help others if he can't even help himself, and sadness at being apparently stuck, never catching that "one big break." In spite of all these things, however, he has committed to let Jesus guide him on the rest of his life's journey. It is not necessary to wait until all our problems are solved before we choose to entrust the future to God and let Jesus be our teacher and guide. If we have to wait for every issue of life to be settled, we'll still be waiting when we're eighty.

Jesus invited ordinary people to follow him and become his disciples. In the beginning, when he called four Galilean fishermen to leave their boats and nets and come with him, he didn't identify any preconditions and he didn't say exactly where the journey would take them, except that it would connect them with other people. He only said, "Follow me, and I will make you fish for people" (Mark 1:17 NRSV). Following Jesus was an unpredictable adventure. Some who were invited went with him eagerly; others said, No, thanks. Some who went stayed with Jesus for a while—for months or even years—but ultimately abandoned him. Perhaps those who first went with him but later deserted him were scandalized by his behavior or his claims or his language.[3] Others remained with him for the rest of his life and all of their own. The affirmation of Simon Peter, printed at

---

3. John 6:21–71, the text that describes Jesus' teaching about himself as the bread of life, is a passage both beautiful and full of profound meaning, but it ends on a wistful note. The people whom he fed with five loaves and two fishes, who had followed him to Capernaum and engaged in dialogue with him, respond negatively to his words (vv. 53–55): "'I am the living bread which came down from heaven; if any one eats of this bread, he will live for ever; and the bread which I shall give for the life of the world is my flesh.' The Jews then disputed among themselves, saying, 'How can this man give us his flesh to eat?' So Jesus said to them, 'Truly, truly, I say to you, unless you eat the flesh of the Son of man and drink his blood, you have no life in you; he who eats my flesh and drinks my blood has eternal life, and I will raise him up at the last day. For my flesh is food indeed, and my blood is drink indeed.'" The Gospel tells us (vv. 66–69), "After this many of his disciples drew back and no longer went about with him. Jesus said to the twelve, 'Do you also wish to go away?' Simon Peter answered him, 'Lord, to whom shall we go? You have the words of eternal life; and we have believed, and have come to know, that you are the Holy One of God.'"

Deciding to Follow Jesus

the heading of this chapter, expresses the conviction of the disciples whose confidence in Jesus had become complete: "Lord, to whom shall we go? You have the words of eternal life; and we have believed, and have come to know, that you are the Holy One of God" (John 6:68–69).

From the New Testament it appears that people were regarded as disciples as soon as they began to follow Jesus. But it also shows there were different circles within the larger group of disciples, some who were actually uncommitted or opportunistic, like the ones who eventually abandoned him, and others who were utterly serious. As best we can tell, in the context of rabbinical practice in Jesus' day, every true disciple was dedicated to reproducing the life of his master. The connection between disciple and teacher was regarded as closer than the bond between parent and child. Such disciples were not merely fans or admirers, nor were they only "students" in the way we generally use the word. Disciples wanted to imitate their teacher and pattern their lives on his as closely as possible.

It's important for those who are coming back to church and those who want to renew their commitment to Christ to understand that the challenges of authentic discipleship (as opposed to nominal church membership) have not changed since Jesus invited the fishermen to leave their boats and nets and come with him. To persevere in following Jesus with sincerity today, just as two thousand years ago, means ultimately to commit oneself to imitating a man whose destiny was to lay down his life for his friends, and who said to those friends, after they had been with him for a while, "If any want to become my followers, let them deny themselves and take up their cross and follow me" (Matt 16:24 NRSV). Eugene Peterson, in *The Message*, paraphrases those words of Jesus this way: "Anyone who intends to come with me has to let me lead. You're not in the driver's seat; I am. Don't run from suffering; embrace it. Follow me and I'll show you how." That was a tall order in AD 29, and it is no less so today.

Clearly there are many people of every age in our churches today who don't take such a lofty and serious view of discipleship. Traditional, nominal church membership feels just fine for them. But I think those who return to the church after a long absence are looking for something of greater seriousness and substance. They want to be more than just church members. And I trust that people who have stuck with the church but now recognize the need to restart their personal journey with Jesus are looking for something beyond the lowest common denominator of church life. Only brave idealists are likely to respond to the invitation to imitate Christ. Those who choose this way of life need to recognize at the outset that the journey to which Jesus invites us, which he once described as the narrow and difficult way that leads to life (see Matt 7:12–14), is not always going to feel like cruising in a new BMW convertible on a sunny, wide-open highway beside the blue Pacific. Instead, it's sometimes going to feel like navigating Manhattan traffic at 4:30 on a rainy Friday afternoon in a Winnebago. Disciples should have no illusions about this way of life or imagine that it promises health, prosperity, success, a lovable spouse, perfect children, and a contented old age. Consider the course of Jesus' own life, or read the lives of the saints of old, or even of the twentieth century. Should we expect something different?

It's important also for returnees and restarts to be fully aware that if they truly seek to follow Jesus rather than simply be church members, they will not progress in just a few months or even a few years from being "beginners" to being "spiritual masters" (to borrow a term from eastern religions). Those who imagine they have become Christian spiritual masters are only demonstrating a form of beginner behavior. One does, indeed, make progress on the Christian path; following Jesus is not a treadmill. But spiritual progress in Christ is not a linear movement from A to B to C; and although there are many well-written and inspirational books available for those who want to keep learning, there is no book—certainly not this one—that can provide perfect guidance for everyone and define exactly what should be done next. Each of us is unique; the right next move for one might not be right for someone else. There's no YouTube video to illustrate three or six or even ten simple steps to a fulfilled and happy Christian life, and there's no course available at the local community college (or the megachurch across town) that will make the journey to union with God easier.

Following Christ on the upward way is a slow process. It's true that we can read about saints of long ago who achieved holiness in what seems like double-quick time (including many in early centuries who were martyred as children). But they're the exceptions, not the norm. For 99.99 percent of us, in every age, following Jesus as his disciple will include setbacks, doubt, frustration, confusion, and long periods of spiritual dryness when prayer feels impossible. Those who want to join this trek should keep in mind that the trail we follow in the steps of Jesus has many switchbacks, sidetracks, and washed-out bridges that will force detours. And if we persevere as disciples, the path will inevitably bring us to a cross, our personal Calvary.

Deciding to Follow Jesus

Walking this way can prove to be harder than learning Japanese, harder than the most strenuous diet we have ever tried, harder than going back to finish college at forty after dropping out at the end of freshman year to get married, and harder than getting in top shape after twenty years of sedentary lethargy. The time may come when completely abandoning the journey with Jesus will feel very attractive, maybe even sensible. But we *can* make this journey of life, and we *can* surmount every obstacle on the way, because Jesus will guide us and help us.

If you're a church returnee or you want to restart your life as a Christian, this probably sounds intimidating. It should. You might wonder how what I've said so far fits with Jesus' invitation, "Come to me, all who labor and are heavy laden, and I will give you rest. Take my yoke upon you, and learn from me; for I am gentle and lowly in heart, and you will find rest for your souls. For my yoke is easy, and my burden is light" (Matt 11:28–29). What I describe may seem neither easy nor light, but spiritual truth is full of paradox. The gospel abounds with paradoxical sayings, such as "the last will be first, and the first last" (Matt 20:16) and "he who loves his life loses it, and he who hates his life in this world will keep it for eternal life" (John 12:25). Michael Casey writes,

> A person on the way toward God cannot expect continual progress or unwavering determination. We wobble along the journey, stumble off the path, find ourselves attracted in other directions, stand still, even regress. This is almost universal experience. What is significant is the strength of the reflex that keeps us bouncing back. There is something we keep returning to: a vision, a dream, a hope. Something gives us the courage to get up after each fall and resume the journey. This is concrete evidence of the Spirit's work, far more potent than any spiritual euphoria.[4]

There is a wonderful upside to the journey with Jesus; so, while I feel compelled to warn readers of the challenges and hardships of the journey, I must also celebrate the rewards. Trusting Jesus and following him makes it possible for a disciple to abandon the prevalent assumption that living the good life requires staying in control, being stronger than other people, making a lot of money, and achieving what the world esteems as success. Learning from Jesus *does*, indeed, give rest to our souls. It yields an interior strength capable of sustaining his followers through the very worst hardships and disappointments life can bring, though it will not eliminate the *pain* of

---

4. Casey, *Toward God*, 122–123.

those experiences. But arriving at the point where we decide to let go, relax the death grip we have on our own destiny, and utterly trust God takes time.

If following Jesus is as difficult an enterprise as I have described, how does anybody ever do it? And, skeptics ask, "What's the real point of it all, anyway? In the end, is being a Christian really any better for me than taking a yoga class at the Y? Or finding a good therapist and getting my psychological wrinkles ironed out?" Yes, indeed it is better.

Coming to know yourself as a beloved child of God and a companion of Christ—what we call "living in the kingdom of God"—is an experience that goes beyond good health or emotional serenity. I'll say more about this later, but it's important for those who are beginning or restarting the journey with Jesus to know that the key to persevering on the trail in his footsteps is not to be found in working harder or mastering arcane spiritual principles; instead it's found in learning how to let go of striving and release ourselves into the hands of God, trusting that every experience in life is a gift, even those that seem at first quite un-gift-like. This takes place as a lengthy process, and therein lies the challenge for twenty-first century Americans who are accustomed to seeing every challenge in life as a problem to be solved right now. As Parker J. Palmer, the Quaker educator and philosopher, puts it, "You don't think your way into a new kind of living; you live your way into a new kind of thinking."[5]

It's probably worth asking whether I want people to follow Jesus because I believe they're going to burn in hell forever if they don't. Some Christians do think that way; in fact, many do. I thought that, too, when I was young. But, as Saint Paul wrote, "When I was a child, I spoke like a child, I thought like a child, I reasoned like a child; but when I became an adult, I put an end to childish ways" (1 Cor 13:11 NRSV). I believe God loves every soul on the face of the earth more than we can even begin to imagine, more than any of us who are parents love our own children or our spouses. And this loving God would *never* condemn you or me to eternal torment because our religion was the "wrong" one, coldly disregarding our heart's desire to find our way to him, know him, and love him. Who could be so cruel? Certainly not God, who said to the prophet Jeremiah, "You will seek me and find me; when you seek me with all your heart" (Jer 29:13).[6]

---

5. Palmer, *Promise*, 60.

6. Two excellent books that address the question of the eternal destiny of people who are not Christians are Willimon's *Who Will Be Saved?* and Bell's *Love Wins*.

The "eternal life" Jesus promised and the "kingdom of God" about which he told so many parables are not experiences for which we must wait until after death. They are aspects of our relationship to God and other people that are available right now. To put it simply, eternal life begins now and lasts forever. That's really what we seek when in the Lord's Prayer we ask, "Thy kingdom come, thy will be done on earth as it is in heaven." The journey of a disciple of Jesus Christ is one whose destination is Christlikeness: life in loving union with God, starting *now*.

Are there other ways than this journey with Jesus, perhaps easier ways, to reach a similar state of holiness and loving, personal knowledge of God? Perhaps Hinduism or Islam or some other spiritual tradition? Maybe. The other great world religions all have wisdom to offer, but I'm agnostic about them. I've read a lot, but I don't really *know* any other ways from firsthand experience. And even if there might indeed be other ways to the same kind of holiness and loving union with God that is the goal of following Christ, I'm pretty sure none of them are going to be less rigorous or demanding than the Christian way. *Nothing of ultimate value is easy or cheap.* It might be simple, but it won't be *easy*.

I don't know about all the possible alternative ways to union with God, but I *do* know something about the Christian way of life, and that's the path I invite others to follow. Here's an analogy—it's not perfect, so don't push it too far—but let's say that as a Christian spiritual guide I'm something like a violin teacher who tells prospective students, "I love the violin, and I've played it all my life. Playing it gives me immeasurable joy. I'd like to help you learn to play the violin, too, so you can experience the same joy I have. Yeah, I can play a few songs on the piano, but I don't really *know* the piano, and I could never teach you how to play it. But, the violin . . . oh, how much I love it! And I'm sure you'll love it, too, once you get started. Would you like some lessons? I won't charge you anything for them."

In the preface, I said I am writing for people who have already decided that Jesus deserves serious attention, and earlier in this chapter, I pointed out that at a moment when his less-committed disciples are abandoning him, Peter speaks for all those who choose to persevere in their loyalty to Jesus when he says, "Lord, to whom shall we go? You have the words of eternal life; and we *have believed, and have come to know*, that you are the Holy One of God" (John 6:67–69, italics added). Contemporary Christians face

Finding the Way

some challenges when we use New Testament vocabulary to describe our own thinking. We need to grasp the various nuances of meaning attached to the verb believe as it is employed in different biblical instances, since it denotes several clearly related but slightly dissimilar things, depending on the context of its use. Because we claim to believe in Jesus, we must be clear about what that means. Therefore, I want to explore five ways the New Testament uses this verb, paying careful attention to its different implications in each case. Four of the five different shades of meaning applied to believe can be illustrated by quotations from the Fourth Gospel.

Since I just quoted one use of believe in Peter's words to Jesus from the end of the sixth chapter of John, I will start there. In this context, "have believed" indicates an early stage in a process that concludes with coming to know. Such believing implies a somewhat tentative, not-yet-certain kind of knowing, similar to what one would mean if one were to say, "I *believed* studying Mandarin in college would prove to be very valuable some day, and since my company moved me to Beijing last year, I *have come to know* I was right." That sort of believing is *an awareness of possibility that progresses to something more certain*, as it did with Peter. We can imagine him saying something like this to Jesus: "Master, we *believed* that you were someone special on the day we started out with you back there on the lakeshore, the time when you told us, 'Follow me, and I will make you fish for people.' You were like nobody we'd ever seen, like no rabbi we'd ever heard! We asked each another, 'Could this carpenter be the Messiah?' And we said, 'Yes, he *could* be. At the very least, he's a prophet.' So we decided to go with you when you asked us to follow you. Time went on, and we stuck with you, and we listened to what you had to say, and we saw the wonderful works you did. At one point I said to the others, 'Nothing has changed my mind about Jesus since day one. In fact, everything I've seen and heard has made me believe that he truly has been sent from God.' Finally, not too long ago, I said to them, 'There's no more doubt in my mind; Jesus is the Messiah, the Son of God, the one our people have been waiting for. I'm sure of it!' And they agreed with me." Peter said that he and the others "had *believed*" and then "had come to *know.*"

Epistemology is the branch of philosophy concerned with ways of *knowing,* asking questions such as, How can we know whether something is true? Anyone who studies epistemology discovers that outside the realm of pure mathematics there is no discipline where absolute proofs are available. In no other discipline is it possible to know beyond doubt whether any propositions are unquestionably true. That means knowing is tough, even for scientists. But the fact is, scientists don't worry about knowing if something is "true"—scientists are satisfied with being able to assert that something is "probable."[7] Richard Feynman was a brilliant and often entertaining Nobel Prize–winning physicist. In an interview with BBC TV in 1981, he said, "I have approximate answers and possible beliefs in different degrees of certainty about different things, but I'm not absolutely sure of anything, and of many things I don't know anything about, I don't have to know an answer."[8]

But in the ordinary world, everybody—whether scientists, pastors, school teachers, or hairdressers—wants to *know* if certain personally significant propositions are really true. If someone were to ask me if my wife loved me, I would say yes without a bit of hesitation. But if the questioner then asked how I *knew* or if I could *prove* it, I would have a problem. What proof could I come up with? Do I simply answer that I know because she says she does? Or do I answer that she sleeps with me? Or that she's nice to me? That she does my laundry? That she puts up with me repeating the same stories over and over? That she reaches out and takes my hand when we're crossing the street, and that makes my heart go pitty-pat? None of these answers proves that my wife loves me, so how can I possibly say that I know she does? A sharp-thinking undergraduate philosophy student could punch holes in all my reasons, but that doesn't matter to me. I *know* that my wife loves me because I know *her*. This is relational knowing, a personal encounter with the Other, with the Sacred, as opposed to the kind of knowledge epistemologists argue about. This is the way we can know God as revealed in Jesus. Richard Rohr describes it this way, "If we go to the depths of anything, we will begin to knock upon something substantial, 'real,' and with a timeless quality to it. We will move from the starter kit of 'belief' to an actual inner *knowing*. This is most especially true if we have ever (1) loved deeply, (2) accompanied someone through the mystery of dying, (3) or stood in genuine life-changing *awe* before mystery, time, or beauty."[9]

---

7. See Allen, *Theology*, 52.
8. Feynman, "Pleasure," n.p.
9. Rohr, *Falling Upward*, 95 (italics in original).

Finding the Way

A second way we observe the verb "believe" used in the New Testament is in relation to the issue of trust, and this usage means *to have confidence in the words, teachings, or promises of Christ.* This is illustrated by what Jesus says to Nicodemus when that seeker of truth comes to visit him under cover of darkness: "If I have told you earthly things and you do not *believe*, how can you *believe* if I tell you heavenly things?" (John 3:12, italics added). When we say that we believe Jesus in this sense, it means we regard Jesus' words as credible and trustworthy. We treat his instructions as valid, and we rely on them. We hear his promises, and we put our confidence in them. This understanding is also illustrated in Mark, the oldest gospel, where in 1:14–15 we read, "Now after John was arrested, Jesus came to Galilee, proclaiming the good news of God, and saying, 'The time is fulfilled, and the kingdom of God has come near; repent, and *believe in the good news*'" (italics added). *Such a reliance and confidence in the words of Jesus is itself an act of faith*, a choice we consciously make, recognizing that we have no absolute proof, no guarantees, and no insurance to protect us in case our confidence is misplaced.

When Joan and I were married we took marriage vows. She said to me, "I take you, Bruce, to be my husband, to have and to hold from this day forward, for better for worse, for richer for poorer, in sickness and in health, to love and to cherish, until we are parted by death. This is my solemn vow."[10] I trusted the vow she made, and I have continued to trust it for a long time. But there are no airtight guarantees, and I have no insurance to protect me in case I ultimately discover that my trust has been misplaced. Trusting my wife's marriage vow is an act of faith. Believing Jesus is the same kind of act. Yes, it is theoretically possible that I could be deceived, but I believe I'm right about Jesus. In fact, I would even say I *know* I'm right. But my knowing is more a confidence of the heart than a confidence of the intellect.

Sticking with the Fourth Gospel, we find in John 20:24–29 two further ways the verb "believe" is used. On the day of the resurrection, Jesus appears inside a locked room where the disciples—minus Thomas—are gathered. When the others report this encounter to Thomas, he replies, "Unless I see in his hands the print of the nails, and place my finger in the mark of the nails, and place my hand in his side, I will not *believe*" (italics

---

10. Book of Common Prayer, The Celebration and Blessing of a Marriage, 427.

added). Thomas's use of "believe" clearly means that he refuses to accept the truth of the other disciples' claim that Jesus has been bodily raised from the dead until he sees the living Lord with his own eyes and touches his wounds with his own hands. The following week, the risen Christ returns to the same people in the same room, and Thomas is among them this time. Jesus confronts Thomas and says, "Put your finger here, and see my hands; and put out your hand, and place it in my side; do not be faithless [*apistos*, "disbelieving"], but believing [*pistos*]."

The Risen One employs "disbelieving" and "believing" in this dialogue with exactly the same meaning Thomas used when he refused to accept the conclusion of his fellow disciples regarding the reality of the physical resurrection. He tells Thomas to reach out and touch his wounds and thus acquire tangible evidence that will lead him to *believe* that Jesus is truly risen in the flesh. But John the evangelist then proceeds to offer us a fresh way of construing what it means to "believe." He portrays Thomas as replying to Jesus' command to touch his flesh not with a logical statement of agreement, such as, "Lord, I now believe that you have risen from the dead," but rather with an adoring exclamation: "My Lord and my God!" Jesus then says to him, "Have you *believed* because you have seen me? Blessed are those who have not seen and yet *believe*" (italics added). At this point in the Fourth Gospel, to "believe" acquires a brand new shade of meaning: *adoring confession of Christ as Lord and God.*

There is a fifth way the verb "believe" is applied by New Testament writers, a way different from the four I have already described—that is, (1) an awareness of possibility that Jesus is the Messiah, which gradually becomes a certain conviction, (2) a believing which indicates confidence in Jesus' words or teaching, (3) a post-resurrection believing that Jesus had risen bodily from the dead, and (4) Thomas's post-resurrection believing which is an act of worshipful devotion. The fifth way is illustrated in Romans 10:14, where Paul asks, "How are they to call upon him in whom they have not *believed*? And how are they to *believe in* him of whom they have never heard?" (italics added). Paul's use of "believe" and "believe in" here means *to trust oneself utterly to Christ*, and this is the principal way Christians use "believe" in a religious sense today.

To return to the example of how I know my wife's love, I would say that because I know her as I do, I also *believe in* her. If I say concerning my wife, "I believe in Joan," I am obviously not saying merely that I believe Joan exists. Her existence is not open to question, at least not by me. When I say, "I believe in Joan," I am saying I have confidence in her, I trust her. In fact, I entrust myself *to* her. If I became seriously ill and was no longer able to think clearly enough to make decisions about my own care, Joan is the person I believe in, the one I trust to make decisions on my behalf. I gladly put my life in her hands. This is what Christian people most often mean when we say that we "believe in Jesus."

I pray that those who read this book will become the kind of disciples who might say to Jesus, as Peter did, "Lord, you have the words of eternal life; *and we have believed, and have come to know, that you are the Holy One of God*" (italics added). Thomas Merton was a disciple who could have said those words. Merton was a Roman Catholic convert in the years just before World War II, soon became a Cistercian monk, and in 1948 published the single most famous book ever written by an American Catholic, *The Seven Storey Mountain*, an autobiography of his youth and conversion. After years in the monastery, Merton came to understand that the itinerary his life's journey was yet to take and the ways he would come to fulfill his calling from God were essentially unknowable in advance. The important thing was to trust completely in God's love and persevere in following Christ as best he was able, one step at a time. A prayer of Merton's, originally inscribed in one of his journals, was first printed in *Thoughts in Solitude* and has since been republished in many places:

> My Lord God, I have no idea where I am going. I do not see the road ahead of me. I cannot know for certain where it will end. Nor do I really know myself, and the fact that I think I am following your will does not mean that I am actually doing so. But I believe that the desire to please you does in fact please you. And I hope I have that desire in all that I am doing. I hope that I will never do anything apart from that desire. And I know that if I do this, you will lead me by the right road, though I may know nothing about it. Therefore I will trust you always though I may seem to be lost and in the shadow of death. I will not fear, for you are ever with me, and you will never leave me to face my perils alone.[11]

---

11. Merton, *Thoughts*, 79.

Deciding to Follow Jesus

This prayer is a soul-baring cry from a man who had already given his life to God for years as a monk. It has appealed to millions of people since it first appeared in print, and I think it touches our hearts because it foregoes all pretense and posturing and disavows any claim to "knowledge," even of his own self. It's an utterly human expression of raw faith and honest uncertainty. But along with the lack of certainty, it confesses an unshakeable conviction: that the one who is praying seeks only to please God and trusts that the authenticity of this intention is going to keep him on the right road. Merton may have been unsure of many things, but of this one thing he was positive: *God is trustworthy and will never abandon us.* Anyone who can pray Merton's prayer with sincerity must know God's love, though he or she may know nothing else.

Merton's faith was grounded in the Bible, the collective experience of the church, the wisdom of the saints, and the continuing work of the Holy Spirit. He was always aware that his quest for union with God necessarily put him in company with a multitude of others, past, present, and yet to come. That same understanding of true discipleship as participation in a vast communal enterprise rather than a purely solitary quest, is conveyed by Stanley Hauerwas and William H. Willimon in their 1989 book, *Resident Aliens*:

> As disciples we do not so much accept a creed, or come to a clear self-understanding by which we know this or that with utter certitude. We become part of a journey that began long before we got here and shall continue long after we are gone. Too often we have conceived of salvation—what God does to us in Jesus—as a purely personal decision, or a matter of finally getting our heads straight on basic beliefs . . . or of having our social attitudes readjusted. . . . Salvation is not so much a new beginning but rather a beginning in the middle, so to speak. Faith begins, not in discovery, but in remembrance. The story began without us, as a story of the peculiar way God is redeeming the world, a story that invites us to come forth and be saved by sharing in the work of a new people whom God has created in Israel and Jesus. Such movement saves us by (1) placing us within an adventure that is nothing less than God's purpose for the whole world, and (2) communally training us to fashion our lives in accordance with what is true rather than what is false.[12]

---

12. Hauerwas and Willimon, *Resident Aliens*, 52.

Finding the Way

I was reared as a child on the Bible's great sacred story of God's love for his world, with its plot and subplots, its characters, its symbols, and its metaphors. Many, perhaps most, who want to follow Christ today lacked a deep exposure to the Bible during their sponge-like, formative years of childhood. They didn't learn the stories of faith as children sitting at their mothers' knees, the grand narrative of creation, sin, judgment, and redemption found in the Hebrew and Christian Scriptures. But people who decide to walk the journey of life following Jesus should soak up the sacred story—internalizing the portrayal of God's will and God's ways that are rendered in the Bible—in order to recognize who they are, who God is, and what God has done and is doing in history through his Son. Those who feel drawn to follow Jesus learn how to find themselves in the biblical story, remembering that in choosing to follow him they are joining an exodus like that of the children of Israel with Moses on the way to the promised land, a caravan which began the journey long ago and will continue moving on until every one of its members arrives in the kingdom. A host of companions is with us on the way.

For Your Reflection

After reading chapter 1, "Deciding to Follow Jesus"

At the end of each chapter are some bullet points under the heading "For Your Reflection." These items are meant to be practical things you can do to help apply what you read in the chapter. Some will be more appealing for one person than another. In most cases, the reflection points will be invitations to answer a question or ponder a specific point connected with the subject matter of the chapter. In other instances, a reflection point will invite you to undertake a specific activity or to pray in a particular way.

- Meet with your pastor or a trusted Christian friend, and tell that person simply and in your own words that you have decided to follow Jesus and why.
- To repent means to think differently, to change your mind. Have you decided to think differently about something? What?
- Discipleship is a commitment to imitate Christ. For your private reflection, name the qualities you see in Jesus that you want to imitate. Pray, and ask God to help you imitate Christ in these ways.
- Jesus said, "If any want to become my followers, let them deny themselves and take up their cross and follow me" (Matt 16:24). What do you think is going to be your "cross?"
- Do you know someone who is at the same point in his or her spiritual life that you are in yours? Meet with that person and share your journey. We need companions on the way.

Chapter 2

Discovering the Bible

[Jesus] told them many things in parables, saying: "A sower went out to sow. And as he sowed, some seeds fell along the path, and the birds came and devoured them. Other seeds fell on rocky ground, where they had not much soil, and immediately they sprang up, since they had no depth of soil, but when the sun rose they were scorched; and since they had no root they withered away. Other seeds fell upon thorns, and the thorns grew up and choked them. Other seeds fell on good soil and brought forth grain, some a hundredfold, some sixty, some thirty. He who has ears, let him hear."

—MATTHEW 13:3-9

AMERICAN CULTURE HAS CHANGED in many ways since I was born and grew up in a Southern town in the middle years of the last century. How can an aging Boomer like me communicate his personal spiritual experiences and pass on his faith to generations whose upbringing and cultural formation were so different from his own? It feels a little like choosing to be a missionary to another world.

Because of my mother's and grandmother's piety, my childhood spiritual formation was centered on the Bible. When I was a preschooler, my mother read something to me nearly every night out of an illustrated Bible story book for children. It was an old book that had once belonged to her mother, probably printed before 1915, and I still remember a fading chromolithograph of families clinging to rafts of logs before they finally drowned in the waters that rose up to float Noah's ark. There still are very handsome and colorful Bible story books for children that tell about Noah, but the modern ones don't include vivid images of drowning mothers attempting to save their babies from the flood.

When I was seven years old, I received a Bible of my very own, an imitation-leather-bound King James Version, with Jesus' words in red letters. Its stories of encounter between human beings and God pervaded the thought-world of my upbringing, and I was not unique. I was a typical child in a town where most of my school friends were being brought up the same way. By the time I was in third grade, we had to answer the roll in Sunday School by reciting a Bible verse from memory. It didn't always have to be a new one, but we weren't supposed to use "Jesus wept" (the shortest verse in the Bible, John 11:35).

I suppose our post–World War II generation was the last to grow up in a society where it was unusual—at least in our part of the country—to meet a person who was unfamiliar with the main stories of the Bible. Our parents made sure we learned those stories, both from the Old Testament and the New, such as Adam and Eve in the garden of the newly born world; Abraham being called by God to leave his home and journey to a far country to receive a heritage; Joseph dreaming amazing dreams; Moses seeing the burning bush and hearing the voice of God, leading the people of Israel out of Egypt, then later receiving the tablets of the law on Sinai; young David with his slingshot killing the giant Goliath and much later becoming Israel's shepherd king; Mary being visited by the angel, then giving birth to God's Son in a stable; Jesus being tempted by the devil, changing water to wine, healing the paralyzed man who had been lowered through the roof, and finally, sweating blood in Gethsemane before he went to the cross; then, years afterward, Paul seeing the Lord on the Damascus road.

As children, we learned those and many other Bible stories, though we couldn't understand them at a very mature level. Nevertheless, being reared on Bible stories did something important for us: *it prepared us to expect that God was going to be involved in our lives.* We were taught that what we were reading in the Bible was "God's word" as spoken to Abraham, or Moses, or Israel, or Jesus' disciples. And our parents and Sunday school teachers made it clear that God's message to those biblical characters was in a sense also a word spoken to us. That idea created for us a kind of expectancy, a situation in which everything we read in the Bible had the potential of touching and affecting our own lives and experience. People who choose to be guided by Christ in the twenty-first century need to discover the same expectancy that God wants to "connect" with them that earlier generations acquired through the biblical formation once routinely given by Christian parents to their children.

I will come back repeatedly to this matter of our *personal experience* of God, because "the reality of God is a continually *experienced* reality, the God not of the philosophers but of Abraham, Isaac, and Jacob, and of many thousands since their day. The God of biblical faith is a God who is known only in the context of a shared and lived experience. Without that experience *God* remains an intellectual abstraction."[1]

The Abraham story (told mostly in Genesis 12–22) had a significant influence on me at a pivotal time in my life and provided both a way of understanding some things that were going on then and an interpretive lens through which I might contemplate future possibilities. The figure of Abraham is vitally important for Jews, Christians, and Muslims because his appearance marks the first clear indication of a *personal relationship* between God and a solitary individual. Abraham became the central character in a religious tradition of wandering, a tradition in which individual pilgrims came to know and experience God in the course of a long journey. In contrast to the gods of paganism, who were always territorial and fixed in place in their shrines or on their holy mountains, the God of Abraham was shown to be a "moving God"—a God whose power was fully exercised everywhere, who knew no limitations, who summoned human beings out of their confined and protected lives into uncertain paths, and whose presence went ahead of them to guide their journey.[2]

I don't think I'm dangerously generalizing from my own experience when I say those who choose to follow Jesus should—sooner rather than later on their spiritual journey—develop a familiarity with Scripture that permits them, ultimately, to find themselves in the sacred story. By "finding themselves in the sacred story" I mean reading, for example, the story of the call of Abraham (Gen 12:2–8) and realizing that God is doing something like this with *me* right now, which is what I did. Or reading Jesus' two little parables about the Treasure Hidden in a Field and the Priceless Pearl (Matt 13:44–46) and saying "That's how I feel about having chosen to follow Christ." Or reading Paul's autobiographical confession and cry of faith (Rom 7:15—8:2) and saying "that's something *I* could have written." When

---

1. Leech, *Experiencing God*, 25–26 (italics added).
2. Ibid., 28.

we discover a place where the sacred story seems to address us personally, we're beginning to hear God with our heart as we read the Bible.

Men and women who want to practice the Christian faith should try to read the Bible seriously. And when I say they should read "seriously," I don't necessarily mean *studiously*, with the assistance of commentaries and scholarly tools. Bible study is extremely worthwhile, but that precise kind of exercise is not what I'm proposing here. The sort of Bible study we do today was impossible before modern times (at least for all except an elite group of scholars). For most of Christian history, when the majority of people were illiterate, and few of those who were able to read could afford their own copies of the Scriptures, private Bible reading or Bible study almost never happened the way it can now. The gathered Scriptures were meant to be read aloud in assemblies for worship, first for Jews before the time of Jesus and then, later, for Christians, who added their own treasured writings in Greek to the older ones written in Hebrew. Most people, with the exception of scribes (and later monks), only heard the Bible read aloud in large gatherings. And, as best we can guess, those who heard it read aloud in synagogue or church later discussed with one another the meaning of passages they heard. R. P. C. Hanson puts it this way: "We must gladly admit that the Bible always has been and still is more than a dry collection of ancient documents. *It was written from faith to faith*. It was intended for the use of a worshipping community, and outside the context of a worshipping community it is inevitably misunderstood, misinterpreted and misapplied."[3]

People in our time begin reading the Bible on their own for a variety of reasons. Some do so out of a sense of duty, which is what I did as a child. Some do so out of curiosity. Other people arrive at a living relationship with Christ through the influence of Christian friends, then later decide to start reading the Bible seriously.

In four decades of ordained ministry, I've known many church members who attended services every Sunday, but told me they never read the Bible on their own. Their only exposure to Scripture came from listening to the portions read as part of the liturgy. In some ways, people like that are similar to the Christians I already mentioned, who lived before the invention of the printing press and never read the Bible on their own, either because they couldn't read or, if they were literate, because there was no conveniently accessible Bible. Unfortunately, people in America today who only encounter Scripture when it is read in church lack a skill which

---

3. Hanson, *Attractiveness*, 24 (italics added).

illiterate people long ago usually possessed; they cannot easily remember what they have heard. Illiterate people in ancient times had to remember what had been told them or read to them because they had no other way to retain the information. Illiterate people in, say, southern France around the year 400, who spoke Latin as their everyday language, listened as the gospel was chanted in their own familiar tongue during the Sunday liturgy and retained much more of what they heard than literate Americans do today after hearing the Bible read aloud in church.

Here's my point. Familiarity with the Word of God in Scripture *is a good thing*. People who want to let Jesus lead them on their journey of life need to learn to read the Bible the way Jesus himself must have read it when he went to the synagogue, unrolled the scroll of the holy book, and turned his mind to the Word of God—that is to say, reverently, reflectively, thoughtfully, and prayerfully. We need not only to become as familiar as possible with the general content of the sacred story, we also need to learn how to include reflection on Scripture as part of our prayers. To this end, it's worthwhile to learn how to practice the ancient Christian discipline of *lectio divina*, Latin for "sacred reading," with its four phases: reading (*lectio*), meditation (*meditatio*), prayer (*oratio*), and contemplation (*contemplation*).[4]

Any serious reading of the sacred story entails personal involvement with it, not merely intellectual agreement with theological propositions that might be extrapolated from it. Personal involvement with Scripture can be dangerous, because it lays us open to unanticipated consequences. For example, in 2 Samuel 12:1–10 we read how King David, a volatile and impulsive man, listens to a parable told by Nathan the prophet and grows so engaged with it that he boils over in righteous indignation. Then the prophet informs him that the evildoer in the story who so enrages him is based on the king *himself*![5] Those who reflect on the sacred story can't begin to understand it unless they agree to accept something that must have been in the minds of biblical writers (and their later editors), "the belief that through the biblical text there comes an inner content which

---

4. The four phases, or "moments," of *lectio divina* do not all take place in one sitting. Reading and meditation generally happen together. Prayer and contemplation usually occur at other times. For those who would like to learn how to practice this ancient approach to sacred reading and prayer, I recommend Michael Casey's book, *Sacred Reading: The Ancient Art of Lectio Divina*. There is also a very practical website called www.lectio-divina.org that can help a beginner get started.

5. See Merton, *Opening*, 43.

challenges the reader and demands of him a personal engagement [and] a decision and commitment of his freedom."[6] This *personal engagement* is what we're looking for.

I am persuaded that, beginning in childhood, Jesus "found himself in the Scriptures" in much the way I have described. Jewish boys in his time learned to read in the local synagogue. It was their schoolroom as well as their house of worship. The texts from which the students learned to read were the very same scrolls read aloud during Sabbath worship. Scrolls were expensive, but a synagogue would have as many of them as it could afford. Nazareth was a small, poor town, and it's quite possible its humble synagogue owned very few scrolls. But we *do* know that along with its scroll of the Torah (the five books of Moses), it at least possessed an Isaiah scroll (Luke 4:16–17). It's possible—though it cannot be proved—that young Jesus spent a good bit of time in the Nazareth synagogue as a boy, standing with the *chazzan* (the keeper of the scrolls) and reading from the Isaiah scroll. This kind of behavior still happens with spiritually serious young people today.

Interestingly, more than half the Scripture quotations attributed to Jesus in the canonical gospels come from Isaiah, which suggests that his hours in the Nazareth synagogue reading the Isaiah scroll affected him deeply. Here's the reason I think this is so. There are four famous passages of poetry in the latter part of the book of Isaiah, known as the "Servant Songs" (Isa 42:1–4; 49:1–6; 50:1–9; 52:11—53:12). The central character of all four is a nameless figure called simply "the Servant of the Lord." In these poems, the Servant has a ministry to God's people characterized by humble, non-violent behavior, prophetic boldness, eagerness to hear and learn from God, and a deep self-sacrificial obedience to God's will, no matter what that obedience might cost him. Isaiah's poems about the Servant of the Lord must have had a decisive influence on Jesus' growing self-understanding. We know the church from its earliest days treated these four Servant Songs as prophecies foretelling the work of Christ, even though Judaism had never understood them as messianic prophecies. The idea that Isaiah's Servant Songs describe the career of the Messiah may well have originated with Jesus himself.

According to Luke 4:11–21, Jesus identified with the prophetic voice of Isaiah when he gave his first sermon at Nazareth at the start of his public ministry, and Matthew's gospel presents Jesus' work as largely a fulfillment

---

6. Merton, *Opening*, 71.

of Isaiah's prophecies. That's two more pieces of evidence for Jesus' "finding himself" in Isaiah.[7] It's possible Jesus may have come to believe his own calling was going to be self-sacrificial as he read about the Servant in 53:5–6: "He was wounded for our transgressions, he was bruised for our iniquities; upon him was the chastisement that made us whole, and with his stripes we are healed. All we like sheep have gone astray; we have turned everyone to his own way; and the Lord has laid on him the iniquity of us all."

When we are able to "find ourselves" here or there in the history of God's interactions with humankind found in the Bible, it means we're beginning to hear the voice of God addressing us as Jesus did. Obviously, this is not going to happen every time we pick up the Bible and read. Many parts of the Bible have never spoken personally to me, but I still read them when they're assigned by the lectionary I follow day by day. I have discovered through a lifetime with the Scriptures that God has a way of surprising me with fresh insights in passages I previously thought were irrelevant. Thomas Merton says the Bible *"raises the question of identity in a way no other book does. . . .* When you begin to question the Bible you find that the Bible is also questioning you. When you ask: 'What is this book?' you find that you are also implicitly being asked: 'Who is this that reads it?'"[8]

Reading the Bible and acquiring familiarity with its great stories gives us the gift of seeing everyday life through a lens that reveals the ordinary as a vehicle of extraordinary meaning. In *A Doorway in Time*, Herbert O'Driscoll writes about his own religious education as a Church of Ireland schoolboy in the 1940s, when Bible stories made him aware of the way God uses commonplace experiences to communicate truth to those with "eyes to see and ears to hear." He says that as a young person reading the Bible he became aware that in its stories

> the ordinary was seen as signifying more than itself. Thus for Amos a plumb line became an image of justice and integrity. Hosea agonized over his failed marriage and conceived the depths of God's love for a People. Jesus watched a woman searching for a coin and saw an image of the kingdom of Heaven. . . . The common attribute of so many lives in the Bible is this ability to see signs. The simple word sign gives us the word significance. . . . Among the few expressions of exasperation we hear from our Lord are those in which he expresses regret at the inability of some to see signs of God's activity in the things happening around them. . . .

7. Much of this material is drawn from Barker, "Isaiah."
8. Merton, *Opening*, 28 (italics in original).

Discovering the Bible

> For Jesus, coins and sheep and fishes and weddings, seeds, a door, a tree, a widow . . . even his own death, all were more than object, incident, event, or experience. All were made into signs and parables and insights so vivid that for two millennia they became the outriders of a kingdom . . . lights that guide us in our fearful voyaging across the terrible crystal seas of mystery . . . that lie between our earthbound humanity and the throne of God.[9]

Certain fundamentalist preachers look at tragic world events, such as the 9/11 attacks or the Asian tsunami of 2004, and see them as signs of God's wrath and displeasure. That's bad theology, in my judgment. However, on our life journey with Jesus it's important to learn how to pay spiritual attention to what is happening around us. God can use ordinary things we see or hear—such as a tender vine slowly climbing up a huge tree, reflections in a pool of water, the happy face of a little child at play, or a song on the radio—to speak to us a word of direction or admonition. Jesus often said, "He who has ears, let him hear" (Matt 13:9).

Even those who are not (yet) Bible readers are probably familiar with the opening verses of the Fourth Gospel,

> In the beginning was the Word [*Logos* in Greek], and the Word was with God, and the Word was God. He was in the beginning with God; all things were made through him, and without him was not anything made that was made. In him was life, and the life was the light of men. The light shines in the darkness, and the darkness has not overcome it. . . . And the Word became flesh and dwelt among us, full of grace and truth; we have beheld his glory, glory as of the only Son from the Father (John 1:1–5, 14).

For Christians the *Logos* of God, meaning God's eternal truth and wisdom, became a human being, Jesus of Nazareth. We call this event the incarnation. For Christians, Jesus the man is the complete and sufficient self-disclosure of God. For roughly thirty-three years, he lived just as we do. He felt pain; he wept; he grieved; he had colds and fever; he became angry; he made mistakes; and he learned new things. Jesus had the same kind of historical and cultural limitations all humans have, and so—like everyone else 2,000 years ago—he did not know the earth revolved around the sun and the moon revolved around the earth; and he never dreamed of

---

9. O'Driscoll, *Doorway*, 77–79.

television sets, automobiles, or the internet. He was 100 percent human. But we believe he was also 100 percent divine—God's Son, God choosing to share our human flesh, God communicating his love for humankind in a direct, personal, fleshly way. This paradox is at the heart of Christian faith, and it teaches something decisively important about God and how God regards us.

Jesus said and did many more things than are described in the Bible (as it says in John 20:30–31 and 21:25). But the significance of Jesus goes far beyond his teachings and works, because the testimony of the church since the day of resurrection is that Jesus is alive and with us always (Matt 28:20), right down to this very moment. It is precisely *because* of its experience of Jesus as risen from the dead that the first Christian communities produced the various documents ultimately compiled, and later canonized, into what we call the New Testament.

Paul wrote that we need to have "the mind" of Christ (1 Cor 2:13; Phil 2:5). That is to say, we must learn to think as Jesus does; we need to see things as he sees them. That said, it becomes essential for those of us who want to make our life journey with Jesus to enter as best we can into Jesus' understanding of God and God's purposes. Obviously that's possible for us only in a limited way. But we can enter into the mind of Christ and think with him—in even a restricted sense—only when we acquire a grasp of the Bible and come to the point where we perceive the whole sweep of the sacred story that it discloses. So, then, what is the subject of this sacred story to which I keep referring?

If one were reading Tolstoy's epic, *War and Peace*, and a friend asked, "What's that big book all about?", the reader could give several possible correct answers. One answer might be that the book concerns five aristocratic Russian families of the early nineteenth century and their stories. Another answer, taking a historical approach, could be that it tells about Napoleon's invasion of Russia in 1812 and the impact that invasion had on tsarist society. Or, adopting a philosophical perspective, the reader might talk about what Tolstoy as a philosopher and religious thinker was trying to communicate concerning life and war, in general. Similarly, those with a purely secular understanding may regard the Bible as merely a collection of random documents, but those with a spiritual understanding perceive a unity, an overarching theme, and a movement from age to age.[10]

---

10. Using Tolstoy's *War and Peace* as an illustration is borrowed from Teague, "Biblical Metanarrative."

Discovering the Bible

The technical word that's used for what I call "the sacred story" is *metanarrative*.[11] The metanarrative of the Bible is the great story the Scriptures tell about God, in particular about how God revealed himself in the past through encounters with individuals and nations, particularly through the people known to history as Israel and the community that formed around Jesus and came to be known as the church. Postmodern thought denies there are any metanarratives, any "big stories," that tie human history together and give it cosmic meaning. Instead, postmodern philosophers assert there can be only a multitude of "little stories," local narratives rather than metanarratives. But despite the pronouncements of postmodernists (and modernists who came before them), Christians assert that the Bible is written testimony to the self-revelation of God to the world, and we perceive both a plot and a direction through the collection of myths, legends, histories, poems, proverbs, prophecies, visions, laws, biographies, letters, and other kinds of documents that make up the Bible. It constitutes a unique witness—to a unique activity of God, to a unique course of events that happened to a unique people, and finally, to a unique Person.[12]

For us, the self-revelation of God reached its culmination in the incarnation, death, and resurrection of Christ, and we see these events as the central interpretive principles of the whole sacred story, the metanarrative of the Bible. If we examine the New Testament, it seems obvious that Jesus believed in what we would call the biblical metanarrative. To choose a single example, in Mark 1:15 we hear Jesus announcing, "The time has come. The kingdom of God is near. Repent and believe the good news!" In saying this, he proclaims that God has been working out his purposes through history, and the reign of God has finally arrived. Jesus understood his own life as a fulfillment of the purposes of God that had been announced long before by the prophets.

---

11. "*Metanarrative* or *grand narrative* or *mater narrative* is a term developed by Jean-François Lyotard to mean a theory that tries to give a totalizing, comprehensive account to various historical events, experiences, and social, cultural phenomena based upon the appeal to universal truth or universal values. In this context, the narrative is a story that functions to legitimize power, authority, and social customs. A grand narrative or metanarrative is one that claims to explain various events in history, gives meaning by connecting disperse events and phenomena by appealing to some kind of universal knowledge or schema. The term grand narratives can be applied to a wide range of thoughts which includes Marxism, religious doctrines, belief in progress, universal reason, and others." *New World Encyclopedia*, "Metanarrative," n.p.

12. Hanson, *Attractiveness*, 21.

Finding the Way

The biblical metanarrative, broadly speaking, shows that human beings must learn how to choose God's ways from among many possible alternatives. In his dealings with us, God draws forth our freedom, initiative, and responsibility. The Bible shows God to be present and active in our mortal affairs, exercising his own choices but not *controlling* our human choices. In the sacred story, instead of manipulating human beings, God promises to be with us as a faithful participant in our lives.[13] Our destiny—*if we will embrace it*—is to live in freedom as "children of God" and "fellow heirs with Christ," choosing to link ourselves with Jesus in his selfless love (see Rom 8:11–18). Merton said,

> If we approach [the Bible] with speculative questions, we are apt to find that it confronts us in turn with brutally practical questions. If we ask it for information about the meaning of life, it answers by asking us when we intend to start living? Not that it demands that we present suitable credentials, that we prove ourselves in earnest, but more than that: *we are to understand life not by analyzing it but by living it in such a way that we come to a full realization of our own identity*. And this of course means a full realization of our relatedness to those with whom life has brought us into an intimate and personal encounter.[14]

Many different voices speak in the sacred story, many different biblical "storytellers." For example, we observe a variety of perspectives on how God uses his authority, depending on which biblical books are under consideration. But we can understand these various perspectives as arrows pointing us toward the cosmic mystery of life in which both divine purpose and human freedom play essential roles.[15] The sacred story shows God as the Creator who has a purpose for his human creatures, but it is a destiny that will only unfold for us in the fullness of time, according to God's design, in a future we cannot yet comprehend, except for one crucial truth: *we are God's own children*. The author of the First Epistle of John put it this way, "See what love the Father has given us, that we should be called children of God; and so we are. The reason why the world does not know us is that it did not know him. Beloved, *we are God's children now*; it does not yet

---

13. These ideas are drawn from the author's notes on a workshop address by Frederick H. Borsch, entitled "The Authority of the Bible," part of the Trinity Institute Conference, *Authority in Crisis*, held at the Roosevelt Hotel in New York, 1988.

14. Merton, *Opening*, 30 (italics added).

15. Borsch, workshop notes, as above.

appear what we shall be, but we know that when he appears we shall be like him, for we shall see him as he is. And every one who thus hopes in him purifies himself as he is pure" (1 John 3:1–3, italics added).

If we ponder the stories Jesus used in teaching the crowds in Matthew, Mark, and Luke, it appears most of his parables were not meant to provide simple answers or "tie everything up with a neat bow"—as we often wish they did—but to challenge hearers and *invite them into the story*, where they might find direction toward God's purposes and partnership with God. In John's gospel, shortly before Jesus' enemies seize him in the Garden of Gethsemane, he tells his disciples, "I have yet many things to say to you, but you cannot bear them now" (John 16:12). Some revelations of Jesus' truth must wait until God's children are better prepared to learn.

A saying usually attributed to the Buddha expresses a profound observation about teaching and learning: "When the student is ready, the teacher will appear." This means that if persons of any age are not ready to learn, it doesn't matter how gifted and well-qualified the teachers trying to communicate with them might be. The students will not learn because they are not *ready* to learn. But when people are ready to learn, suddenly it seems they're encountering brilliant teachers every day. Something similar might be said about readiness to hear God speaking to us in the words of Scripture. Getting us ready to hear is the work of the Holy Spirit. When we're finally ready to hear, we will experience God addressing us time after time.

Finding the Way

For Your Reflection

After reading chapter 2, "Discovering the Bible"

- If you don't own a Bible that seems readable to you, go to a bookstore and buy one. (Appendix B, "Bibles and Bible Reading," p. 165, suggests a variety of possibilities.) You might borrow several from the public library or a church library and try them out before you decide which one you like. I think the best contemporary American English version is the paraphrase by Eugene Peterson, entitled *The Message*. (You might also ask a Bible-reading friend to make a suggestion.)

- If you are not already in the habit of reading Scripture, decide on a reading plan that seems as if it might work for you, given your work schedule and family responsibilities. There are many Bible reading plans available online, and there are also suggestions in appendix B.

- As you read the Bible (following whatever plan you choose) keep a simple notebook or journal where you write down verses or stories that seem to speak to you, especially stories where you can see yourself in one of the characters. Make a note when you think you've learned something new or important.

- Before you begin reading the Bible, ask God to "speak" to you in a way that you can understand. Trust that God wants you to hear him.

- Are there verses from the Bible (or stories or parables) that already have a personal significance for you? Make a list. Memorize one of the verses or learn to retell a story or parable in your own words.

- When you go to church on Sunday, listen carefully to each reading from the Bible. Do not follow along in a printed copy, but just listen. (Every book of the Bible was written to be read aloud.) After you have listened carefully to the reading, think about whatever stuck in your mind; don't worry about the parts that didn't stick. From what you know about Jesus from the Bible, how would you say Jesus perceived the world?

Chapter 3

Experiencing God's Love

Beloved, let us love one another; for love is of God, and he who loves is born of God and knows God. He who does not love does not know God; for God is love. In this the love of God was made manifest among us, that God sent his only Son into the world, so that we might live through him. In this is love, not that we loved God but that he loved us and sent his Son to be the expiation for our sins. Beloved, if God so loved us, we also ought to love one another. No man has ever seen God; if we love one another, God abides in us and his love is perfected in us.

—1 JOHN 4:7-12

IN THE LAST CHAPTER, I wrote about my Bible Belt upbringing. That was when I—along with millions of other small children—learned to sing, "Jesus loves me, this I know, for the Bible tells me so." As a child, I must have heard ten thousand times that God loves me, but I was an adult, with a pretty thorough grounding in the Bible, before the *feeling* of being loved by God came to fill my heart and move my frequent vocal affirmations of divine love from the realm of theological confession into the realm of personal experience.

The Bible tells us about the love of God in more places than I can list. The best-known text describing God's love is John 3:16. Many people in America who have never attended a church service and have no interest in Christianity know about John 3:16. They read it many times splashed in large letters on billboards beside highways, printed on bumper stickers, and hand-lettered on signs held up by fans at football games: "God so loved the

Finding the Way

world that he gave his only Son, that whoever believes in him should not perish but have eternal life."

Love is a confusing word because we use it for many different purposes in contemporary American discourse. Love can describe trivial attachments ("I just *love* that song") as well as name the most serious life relationships ("I *love* my wife so much"). Therefore, when someone says "God loves you," it's legitimate to ask exactly what is meant. To start with, God's love for us has to be *perfect love*. Since it comes from God, it obviously can't be a trivial attachment; that would be ruled out. Furthermore, because God's love is perfect, it also can't be one of the perversions of love which characterize some human behavior—displays of affection and attention that are really infatuation, obsession, manipulation, or exploitation.

God *chooses* to love us. The love God offers is not a response to lovable qualities he discerns in us. In fact, God loves people who have no lovable qualities anyone can observe. And God does not love us because we love him. He loves people who have never given him a moment's thought. We may accurately say God's love for us proceeds from a divine *decision*, but it's a decision as inherent to God's nature as the decision to breathe is inherent to our nature. Indeed, John goes so far as to say "God is love" (1 John 4:16b). In John's eyes, God's love defines God's very being. We might even say God created us to receive his love; that is our *raison d'être*.[1]

God's love for us is a unique kind of love. It's not like friendship, which grows out of familiarity and shared interests. God's love is not like sexual desire, characterized by a passionate, physical yearning for the other. It's also not like the emotional attachment we develop for familiar things or places. What, then, *is* God's love like? To what can we compare it?

We have to believe the writers of the New Testament chose their words carefully. They were writing in Greek, and that language has four different

---

1. The New Testament teaches that God is love, and divine love requires objects to love. Author and essayist Joel J. Miller has an essay entitled, "God made us to love us" (www.patheos.com), in which he writes the following: "The Father, Son, and Holy Spirit live in a relationship of eternal and mutual love. But, as fourth-century theologian Gregory Nazianzen observes, it is the nature of love to seek objects to love. For an uncreated God, that means it is natural to create. 'Good must be poured out and go forth,' said Gregory, beyond the Holy Trinity itself, 'to multiply the objects of Its beneficence.' . . . This is an exciting truth: God made us to bless us, to love us. Sometimes we assume that we were created to serve, love, and worship him. These are good and holy actions, but they are *responses* to God's *initiating* act of love. He did not require service, love, and worship, and so created servants, lover [sic], and worshippers. God's only requirement is to be himself, to love. We are born—all things are born—from that divine desire."

Experiencing God's Love

words that are all translated into English by the single word love.² New Testament writers deliberately used a specific Greek verb, *agapaō* (and its corresponding noun, *agapē*), to speak of the love of God. In nonreligious Greek usage *agapaō/agapē* were words applied in a variety of contexts, including expressions of satisfaction with a meal or honor for a guest or preference for one thing over another.³ It is possible that the widespread use of *agapaō/agapē* in ordinary Greek to indicate choice or preference might have led New Testament writers to use that word to name the love God chooses to bestow on us—*love that is an act of the will*, not an involuntary emotional response to circumstances.

God's love for us is a gift, a gift undeserved by the recipients. We might say the purpose of God's becoming human in Jesus—the event we call the incarnation—was to convey to humankind the reality of divine love in a way that would communicate clearly to anyone. We can only construe God's becoming a vulnerable man as a sign of God's amazing love. He chose to endure all the possible pains and disappointments that go along with being human, including physical and psychological abuse, rejection by his best friends, and, finally, death at the hands of his enemies. John 3:16 says, "God so loved the world." Perhaps we can accept that God loves *the world*. The greater challenge for most of us is to embrace God's love on such an intimate level that it compels us each to exclaim, "God loves *me!*"

However, if we tell others "I know God loves me," we can count on probing, argumentative questions being asked, such as "*How* do you know? How can you be *sure* God loves you?" Questioners will remind us of events that did not work out happily for us, such as losing a job, or becoming critically ill, or experiencing the death of a loved one, and—if they run true to type—the questioners will at some point ask, "If God loves you so much, why did he let that happen to you?"

The answer I give to the question "How can you know God loves you?" is not different from my answer to the question "How do you know your wife loves you?" My answer is that I know in my heart that my wife loves me, even though I can't prove it with a technically indisputable argument. The same answer applies to the question about how I can know God loves me. I know my wife loves me because I know *her*; and I know God

---

2. See Lewis, *Four Loves*. Lewis expounds upon the differences between *storgē*, which he calls "affection," *philia*, which he calls "friendship," *eros*, which he simply calls "eros" (or "being in love"), and *agapē*, which he calls "charity." All four Greek words are all usually translated with the single English word *love*.

3. See Quell and Stauffer, "*Agapaō*," 36.

loves me because I know *him*. I have a relationship with God. That's not a philosophical answer, it's a "heart answer" arising from the faith with which I've lived my life.

As to the antagonistic question about how a loving God can permit his beloved to suffer, the question itself is intellectually shallow and the answer is simple. It is self-evident that suffering has a part to play in human life and growth. Parents who shield their offspring from every pain and problem as they are growing up ultimately have troubled, immature, and pathologically needy adult children on their hands. The mystery of suffering is woven into the nature of creation; we learn more through adversity than we do through pleasure. The author of the Letter to the Hebrews even wrote that God's Son was made "perfect through suffering."[4] God's promise to us is not that he will protect us from suffering, loss, or grief, but that he will always be with us, even in the midst of our pain. In his Letter to the Romans, Paul said, "We know that in everything God works for good with those who love him, who are called according to his purpose" (Rom 8:28). As Thomas Merton's well-known prayer says, "I will trust you always though I may seem to be lost and in the shadow of death. I will not fear for you are ever with me, and you will never leave me to face my perils alone."[5]

Although the Bible is the written testimony to God's self-revelation in history, most of us—and I include myself in this—best understand what we read in the Bible when we're able to use analogical imagination to make connections between Scripture and our personal experience. Analogies are more illuminating to us than are dissertations on the social history of Judea in the time of Christ or different possible translations of Greek words, even if we've had a formal theological education. In many sermons over the years, I have assured listeners that we are all God's children and God loves us more than we can imagine. Those sermons were all expositions of New Testament passages, but I *understand* those passages best through the application of my own personal analogy: the interpretive lens of my experience as a father of four children whom I have loved all their lives. Here's one of those experiences.

My first child was born in 1972. Shortly after he was born a nurse handed him to me, saying "Daddy, it's time for you to hold this little guy."

---

4. "For it was fitting that he, for whom and by whom all things exist, in bringing many sons to glory, should make the pioneer of their salvation perfect through suffering" (Heb 2:10).

5. Merton, *Thoughts*, 79.

Experiencing God's Love

I sat down, and she put my newborn son on my lap, wrapped tightly in a receiving blanket with a little knit cap on his head. I sat there, holding him and looking down into his scrunched-up, small red face, and I was overwhelmed with how much love I felt for this child—*my* child.

I was not quite twenty-seven years old, and I was emotionally overcome in a way I had not expected to be, though in the years since then, I have learned from other dads that such feelings are very common. I loved my newborn little boy with all my heart, even though he'd only been in the world an hour. He had not yet said a word; he had not yet achieved anything; he hadn't hit a home run or made straight As. But I loved him absolutely and unconditionally just because he was my child. And as I sat in a straight-backed hospital room visitor's chair cuddling this little bundle, the voice of God spoke clearly in my imagination, saying, "That's how I feel about *you*, just because you're *my* child!" Those few moments in the hospital room with my firstborn were worth more to me than any amount of advanced New Testament study. The sense that I am God's child, dearly loved and intimately known by my heavenly Father, was imprinted on my soul from that moment on.

I can only tell this story from a paternal perspective, but I know mothers feel at least the same way and probably even more passionately. There is no more powerful human love than mother-love. We do well to remind ourselves that the Bible, though written in a patriarchal culture and using predominantly masculine metaphors in speaking of God, also applies very vivid maternal images both to God "the Father" and to Jesus Christ "the Son."[6] As Julian of Norwich observed in the fourteenth century, God is our Mother, too.[7]

Of course, when my first child was born and I felt such a great outpouring of love for him, *he* could not feel it. It was up to me to communicate my love to him (and later to my younger children) through the life we shared. That's what we Christians believe God was doing in the incarnation,

---

6. See Isa 49:5; 66:13; and Matt 23:37, in which Jesus compares himself to a mother hen. See also Leech, *True Prayer*, 21–24. According to Leech, the feminine element in the Holy Spirit is emphasized in Syrian patristic sources, and Clement of Alexandria even writes of Christians "feeding from the breast of the *Logos*."

7. "Jesus Christ that doeth good against evil is our Very Mother: we have our Being of Him,—where the Ground of Motherhood beginneth,—with all the sweet Keeping of Love that endlessly followeth. As verily as God is our Father, so verily God is our Mother; and that shewed He in all, and especially in these sweet words where He saith: *It is I.*" Julian of Norwich, *Revelations*, 125.

life, death, and resurrection of Jesus: *God was communicating his love to us.* He was engaging us personally in a way that would permit us to perceive the depth of his love. The Gospel according to John reports that Jesus said, "I and the Father are one" and "he who has seen me has seen the Father" (John 10:30 and 14:9b). I imagine Jesus might well have added something like this as he spoke to his disciples: "My friends, if you want to know what God is like, look at me! If you want to know how God feels about you, observe how much *I* love you!"

There are certain mental pictures that help me understand and explain who God is and who I am in relationship to God. For example, I imagine myself as a young child, perhaps kindergarten age, who has a loving, wise, and empathetic Father—God—whose character and "personality" have been disclosed by Jesus. My image of myself as a young child in relationship to God derives from an episode in the ministry of Jesus when he was teaching in public, and people were bringing their small children to him for a blessing. Jesus' disciples tried to stop the parents from bringing their children to him, presumably because they thought the presence of children would interrupt the serious instruction Jesus was giving. But, as it turned out, the presence of infants and toddlers provided Jesus with an opportunity to teach his listeners something important. Mark tells the story this way: "They were bringing children to him, that he might touch them; and the disciples rebuked them. But when Jesus saw it he was indignant, and said to them, 'Let the children come to me, do not hinder them; for to such belongs the kingdom of God. Truly, I say to you, whoever does not receive the kingdom of God like a child shall not enter it.' And he took them in his arms and blessed them, laying his hands upon them" (Mark 10:11–16).

Jesus told the people around him, including the disciples who had been trying to make the parents keep their children away from him, "Whoever does not receive the kingdom of God like a child shall not enter it." The biblical expression "kingdom of God" is complex and multi-dimensional, used in a variety of ways in both the Old Testament and the New. Here, it refers not so much to a special zone of God's sovereignty as to a *special relationship with the sovereign God,* which can only be received from him as a gift. This is a relationship that amounts to much more than simply being under the authority of God, since all Creation is by definition already subject to God's authority. "Receiving the kingdom of God" must mean *having an experience that brings one to sharp awareness of an intimate relationship with God.* I believe Jesus used "the kingdom of God" here to indicate what we might otherwise call "the family of God"—including everything a family relationship would entail in terms of privileged access to God and a future as one of God's children. Paul later wrote that this special status in relationship to God was that of being "heirs of God and fellow heirs with Christ" (Rom 8:17).

In the first chapter of John's gospel, describing the incarnation of the eternal Word, the gospel writer says, "He came to his own home, and his own people received him not. But *to all who received him, who believed in his name, he gave power to become children of God*; who were born, not of blood nor of the will of the flesh nor of the will of man, but of God" (John 1:11–13, italics added). Two chapters later in the same gospel, Jesus tells the Jewish elder Nicodemus that to enter the kingdom of God, one must be "begotten from above," which is exactly what I'm talking about (John 3:3, 7).[8] One must become God's child—and I mean God's *little* child. Growth to maturity as sons and daughters of God occurs as we pass our lives in a personal relationship with him.

This brings us back to the episode when parents were bringing their children—obviously very young ones—to Jesus, so he could take them in his arms and lay his hands on them in blessing. What characteristics of children did Jesus have in mind when he said, "Whoever does not receive the kingdom of God *like a child* shall not enter it"? No certain single answer can be given, of course, but the question invites us to meditate on what it might mean for us to become "like a child."

Jesus could have meant that—regardless of anyone's age or education or social status—each of us needs to reawaken some essentially childlike qualities if we want to receive what God has in store for us. So I ask myself: What are the qualities I once possessed as a child that I need to rediscover in order to be in a right relationship with God as my Father? And, by the way, I'm quite sure God's kingdom is already here among us. Taking our

---

8. See Brown, *Gospel*, 128. According to Brown, Jesus' statement to Nicodemus is best translated: "No one can see the kingdom of God without being *begotten from above*" (italics added). Brown explains that "Begotten from above" more accurately renders the Greek phrase *gennēthē anōthen* than do the usual translations, "born again" and "born anew." The Greek word *gennēthē*, which is used in John 3:3 and 3:7, is a form of the word that can specifically apply to the role of the father in the birth of a child, making it particularly applicable if the thought behind the expression is that God becomes one's Father.

place in it is not just about "going to heaven," rather it's about claiming a way of life that's available to us through the love of God now.

The first and most obvious characteristic of the infants whose parents were bringing them to Jesus was that they *had nothing of their own except what they had received from their parents*. Their physical appearance, their clothing, their playthings—all were, in some sense, gifts. This is true of our own children and grandchildren. Those of us who are parents know one of a small child's first and most frequently used words is "mine!"—usually expressed stridently while snatching a favorite toy out of the hands of a sibling. But if asked who gave her that doll, the child would certainly say, "Mommy" or "Grandma" or someone else. She is not going to say, "Nobody gave it to me. I made it (or bought it) myself." We might say a fundamental characteristic of little children is that they know everything they receive is in some sense a gift. *Do I accept my life, in all its dimensions, as a gift from God, including my education, my achievements, my possessions, and whatever status I might have?*

Something else we can observe about normal small children is that they're spontaneous. They live in the moment. They don't worry about what didn't get done this morning. They aren't anxious about what has to be done this afternoon. To enter the kingdom of God today, you and I must rediscover our capacity for spontaneity and joy. *Can I be as free-spirited again now, in my serious adulthood, as I was at the age of four?*

Another characteristic of young children is that *they have no doubt about their importance to their parents* (or grandparents). For example, I can be sitting in my favorite chair watching a baseball game on TV, but if a grandchild comes and crawls up in my lap, I don't put the child down because she is blocking the TV. I love it when one of our grandchildren wants to sit on my lap. To enter the kingdom of God, we have to believe that we're just as important to our heavenly Father as our own little children or grandchildren are to us. We're God's children, and we can crawl up and sit in our Father's lap, figuratively speaking, any time we want (even if we're well over seventy). I do it, and I recommend it to everyone. We only have to use our imaginations, which is a precious gift most of us unfortunately suppress as we get older. *Can I trust that I, a sinner, might be cherished in such a way by God?*

Something more about children that we need to imitate if we're to enter the kingdom of God is their *absolute confidence in the future*. When I was in seminary forty-plus years ago, I worked in a parish in the South Bronx. If somebody asked poor, inner-city ten-year-olds back then or similar kids today what they are going to be when they grow up, they'd say, "I'm going to be a doctor" or "a ballerina"—or an astronaut, or a pro basketball player, or an explorer, or a pop singer—*anything*! Little children believe in their own limitless possibilities. They're confident they will be able to do anything, be anything. They believe in the future. It's full of hope for them. Jesus says in Mark 10:27 that the kingdom of God belongs to those who become like children, children who know that "with God all things are possible." All things. *Do I believe in my possibilities?*

Young children are aware there are many things they don't know. That's why, once they're able to talk, children are so full of questions—*What's that? Where did it come from? What does it do?* and, especially, *Why?* They're conscious that they have a lot of growing to do and a lot to learn. And the first people to whom children instinctively turn for answers, and whose answers they trust absolutely, are usually their mothers and fathers. *Do I realize that in the divine scheme of things I am just a little child? Am I able to be as teachable as a child? Do I trust God to reveal to me, in his own time and in his own way, many things that are as yet incomprehensible to me?*

The last quality common to young children that Jesus might have been thinking about is *the awareness of many things they cannot do for themselves.* Little children are dependent. We know they're dependent on adults, and they know it, too—even if they often wish it were not so. Little ones say, "I can do it by myself!" A four- or five-year-old thinks he wants to be "big" and independent. That's perfectly natural. But small children usually know what they can do right now and what they can't. *Am I able to let myself be dependent on God, especially if that translates into letting myself depend on other people?*

Unless we become like little children, we cannot enter the kingdom of God. That is, we cannot partake of the heritage meant for us as sons and daughters of God. But if we can become childlike, we can climb into our heavenly Father's lap, look into his eyes, and tell him we want to be part of what he's doing in our world—right now, today, this minute. And then we can receive that privilege from him as a gift. What Jesus called "the kingdom of God" is beyond our ability to earn or achieve, but—paradoxically—it's within our grasp if we're willing to accept it from our Father's hand *as a gift*, not an entitlement.[9]

If we understand ourselves to be God's beloved children and accept that God chooses to love us with the unconditional love of a mother or a

---

9. The substance of this exposition of Mark 10:11–16 is found in McNab, *Let Your Light Shine*, 221–231. Some imagery is from Campolo, "If I Should Wake," n.p.

father for a beloved child, we will have a kind of security nothing else can offer. When we perceive the reality and depth of such love, it *changes our hearts*. It changes the way we think about other people, too. But if we think of God as a critical parent—perpetually finding fault with us, withholding love from us, or punishing us for our failure to live up either to his expectations or our own potential—then we're not going to have a joyful relationship with God. And we're not going to have the best possible relationships with other people, either.

Jesus consistently speaks of God in an intimate way as his Father, and he invites those who follow him to do the same. You might be surprised to know that *only* Christianity explicitly invites people to think of God as their Father. Some non-Christians hear the words of Jesus from John 14:6, "I am the way, and the truth, and the life; no one comes to the Father, but by me," and feel offended because they think Jesus was claiming to offer the only path to God. Jews, Muslims, Hindus, and others intend to offer paths to God.[10] But we should take note of exactly what Jesus said. His words were "No one comes to *the Father* except by me." He did not say "no one comes to *God* except by me." Jesus called God his *Abba*. (*Abba* was the familiar name Jewish children used in speaking to their fathers. The best English equivalent is "Daddy.") That is how Jesus addressed the Father in prayer (Mark 14:36), just as it had undoubtedly been the name he used for Joseph during his childhood in Nazareth. Use of such a familiar, intimate name for God was unprecedented, perhaps even shocking to some. The Jewish Scriptures never speak of God as *Abba*. This new way of relating to God was drawn by Jesus from his own experience. Later, Paul wrote, "all who are led by the Spirit of God are children of God. For you did not receive a spirit of slavery to fall back into fear, but you have received a spirit of adoption. When we cry, '*Abba*! Father!' it is that very Spirit bearing witness with our spirit that we are children of God, and if children, then heirs, heirs of God and joint heirs with Christ—if, in fact, we suffer with him so that we may also be glorified with him" (Rom 8:14–17 NRSV).

The gospels show Jesus praying to his *Abba*, and the model prayer he taught his disciples is addressed (in English) to "Our Father." This language clearly presumes the relationship between a beloved child and an approachable, loving Father. Judaism teaches a profoundly personal relationship

---

10. I don't mention Buddhism here, since it is a non-theistic religion.

between God and his people and speaks of God as "Father," but not often, and those instances never make use of the more intimate word, *Abba*. "Father" is not one of the ninety-nine names for Allah in Islam, where the Qur'an portrays the divine relationship with human beings as master and servants. Hinduism has thousands of gods, all of which are thought of as manifestations of Brahman, and some of them must have fatherly or motherly aspects. But we have to conclude that only Jesus, and only the Christian religion, proposes that we should come to know God mainly as our Father, our *Abba*, and one another as sisters and brothers of the Son of God who—according to John's gospel—told Mary Magdalene outside the empty tomb on the day of resurrection, "Go and tell my brothers that I am ascending to my Father and their Father, to my God and their God" (John 20:17 NRSV). The paths to God that other religions offer lead no one to that personally intimate, relational knowledge of God as our *Abba* that Jesus invites us to share with him.[11]

All of us have different experiences with our fathers and mothers. Not all fathers are loving and kind; not all mothers are gentle and unselfish. Some of us have experiences with our fathers (or mothers, or both) that leave us with a mental picture of God as either a legalistic, nit-picking judge or an autocrat demanding perfect obedience to all the family rules. If such experiences do not turn us away, as adults, from any desire to think of God as "Father," they might still leave us with the anxious feeling that we're living under the all-seeing eye of a critical God who could suddenly decide that he is offended by our behavior—or even our thoughts—and so condemn us to eternal punishment. We all know people who were brought up with a picture of God as a terrifying deity of wrath and judgment, but I doubt that's the way Jesus wants us to think about God.

In 1 John 4:18, we read, "There is no fear in love." The fear of God about which the Old Testament speaks in many places is not a form of terror but rather a sense of awe coupled with dread. To feel *dread* is not always a bad or scary thing. There's a sense in which we who know ourselves to be deeply loved by God should have a dread of disappointing God. This is similar to the way we feel about disappointing our mother or father, or a special mentor, or a best friend who believes in us and loves, helps, and encourages us. We don't want to let people down who care so much for us, not because they might punish us for our failure or start withholding

---

11. See Leech, *True Prayer*, 22.

affection, but because we want somehow to repay the support and love of these special people by living up to the potential they encourage in us.

Psalm 103:14 says God "knows whereof we are made." That is to say, God knows our frailty and our propensity to be distracted by many things. He knows our positive potential and the gifts he has given us, and he knows our flaws, too. God's love for us is not a love grounded in unrealistic optimism, but in a thorough comprehension of both our true potential and our genuine limitations. As was inscribed on a plaque someone gave me years ago, "God knows all about us but loves us just the same." We can be secure in such love. If we fail to fulfill our potential, if we have a great opportunity and somehow manage to blow it, God is not going to turn away from us in disappointment and give up on us. But such steadfast faithfulness to us does not mean God will therefore shield us from the consequences of our failures. We may well experience suffering, loss, or pain because of our own shortcomings, but God will be with us in our pain and give us the resources to grow through it.

The sacred story found in the Bible includes the life of David, the greatest king of Israel, and it says he was a man after God's own heart (see Acts 13:22). Those words suggest God favored David the shepherd boy, the youngest and least accomplished among eight sons of one father, and saw in him the qualities he wanted in the ruler of his people. But despite being God's chosen king, David later proved himself capable of pettiness, vengefulness, deceit, murder, and even sexual predation. He was morally imperfect; and he suffered during his life in many ways because of his all-too-human failings. We can read the history of David in 1 and 2 Samuel and see how God punished him for his sins. But as the well-known story of David is spun out, we observe that David never failed to acknowledge those sins and seek God's forgiveness; and God never abandoned him. To me, the message of the gospel is that *all of us* are "Davids" in this life: chosen by God and never to be abandoned by him, but nevertheless vulnerable to the consequences of our bad choices. If we go back through the patriarchal history in the book of Genesis, we can see that Abraham, Isaac, and Jacob also were fallible human beings, like David later turned out to be, but nevertheless they were chosen by God and "blessed to be a blessing."

Jesus' story about the rich farmer and his two sons, usually called the parable of the Prodigal Son (Luke 15:11–32) is a peerless portrayal of the love of God. Since the details of the parable of the Prodigal Son might not

Experiencing God's Love

be completely familiar to all readers, here is the full text of Luke 15:11–32, from the NRSV:

> And [Jesus] said, "There was a man who had two sons. The younger of them said to his father, 'Father, give me the share of the property that will belong to me.' So he divided his property between them. A few days later the younger son gathered all he had and traveled to a distant country, and there he squandered his property in dissolute living. When he had spent everything, a severe famine took place throughout that country, and he began to be in need. So he went and hired himself out to one of the citizens of that country, who sent him to his fields to feed the pigs. He would gladly have filled himself with the pods that the pigs were eating; and no one gave him anything. But when he came to himself he said, 'How many of my father's hired hands have bread enough and to spare, but here I am dying of hunger! I will get up and go to my father, and I will say to him, "Father, I have sinned against heaven and before you; I am no longer worthy to be called your son; treat me like one of your hired hands."' So he set off and went to his father. But while he was still far off, his father saw him and was filled with compassion; he ran and put his arms around him and kissed him. Then the son said to him, 'Father, I have sinned against heaven and before you; I am no longer worthy to be called your son.' But the father said to his slaves, 'Quickly, bring out a robe—the best one—and put it on him; put a ring on his finger and sandals on his feet. And get the fatted calf and kill it, and let us eat and celebrate; for this son of mine was dead and is alive again; he was lost and is found!' And they began to celebrate. Now his elder son was in the field; and when he came and approached the house, he heard music and dancing. He called one of the slaves and asked what was going on. He replied, 'Your brother has come, and your father has killed the fatted calf, because he has got him back safe and sound.' Then he became angry and refused to go in. His father came out and began to plead with him. But he answered his father, 'Listen! For all these years I have been working like a slave for you, and I have never disobeyed your command; yet you have never given me even a young goat so that I might celebrate with my friends. But when this son of yours came back, who has devoured your property with prostitutes, you killed the fatted calf for him!' Then the father said to him, 'Son, you are always with me, and all that is mine is yours. But we had to celebrate and rejoice, because this brother of yours was dead and has come to life; he was lost and has been found.'"

Finding the Way

This is probably the best known of all the parables. We can read it as an allegory: the Father in the story clearly represents God; the Prodigal Son represents rebellious and sinful people; and the Elder Brother represents good, proper people who always do the expected thing and keep all the rules. In the story Jesus tells, the Father demonstrates his unshakeable love for both of his sons: first for the Prodigal, who had demanded his inheritance and then wasted it—but comes back home remorseful, hoping to be received as, at best, a hired hand, not a son—and then for the Elder Brother, who is so wrapped up in pride and self-righteousness that he cannot share his Father's happiness at the return of his errant younger brother. He refuses even to call him "my brother," referring to him instead as "this son of yours." Even though their Father tells him "it was fitting to make merry and be glad, for this your brother was dead, and is alive; he was lost, and is found," the sour Elder Brother cannot get over the bitter resentment of what he has chosen to regard as unfair treatment by his Father, despite the fact that the Father has remained constant in his love, acceptance, and provision for his older son and heir. This is a truly amazing story from the lips of Jesus, and many people have rightly said it would be better for us to call it the parable of the Loving Father rather than the parable of the Prodigal Son. This is the God who loves you and me. This is the God who came into our world as a man named Jesus to lead us out of our willful foolishness and alienation into the kingdom of God. How could one not be drawn to such a God?

The late Irish Anglican bishop R. P. C. Hanson was an erudite scholar of early Christian doctrine who claimed to distrust any history written concerning periods subsequent to AD 600. He wrote a book in the early 1970s (from which I have already quoted) with the wonderful title *The Attractiveness of God*. I like the book's title because I think the nature of God, as Jesus discloses it, is immensely attractive. In this learned but also frequently humorous work, Bishop Hanson laid out a compelling argument for Christian faith. He wrote,

> *God moves us with the power of love. The motive-power in Christian belief is the attraction of God's love.* This is not a new discovery of trendy modern theologians. Paul and Augustine knew it long ago, and so have millions of Christians, famous and obscure, ever since, whether they could express their knowledge or not. At the heart of the gospel is the paradoxical, extraordinary, love of God, declared and expressed in his Son Jesus Christ who chose to be born as a man among us, to live a life of unselfishness, and to die a voluntary

Experiencing God's Love

> death by crucifixion for us. This love, vindicated and fully revealed at the resurrection, is what keeps Christianity going. . . . It discloses an endlessly resourceful and compassionate God, always one jump ahead of us, capable of producing a situation which reverses our values and overthrows our conventional religion and leaves us bankrupt before him, able to use evil for good purposes, never at a loss to retrieve the most apparently hopeless situation, nor allergic to acting in history, not so aloof as to be incapable of suffering, but above all continually master of the situation and because he is a loving God, completely trustworthy. These are the ingredients of the attractiveness of God, and this is why I, with many others, find belief in him an irresistibly attractive proposition.[12]

Further on, Hanson adds,

> Ultimately the motive for our being Christians and behaving as Christians—that is to say enduring a good deal of heart-searching and discouragement and difficulty over prayers and disgust with ourselves and consultation with others—is the attractiveness of God. . . . *Ultimately the motive of our being Christian is that we cannot resist the love of God, a love which is not merely a declaration nor a message nor an appeal, but a mighty act of self-giving, undeserved, unexpected, unasked and embarrassingly generous.*[13]

Our generous and loving God, our *Abba*, draws us to himself. He wants us to open our hearts willingly and fearlessly to him. Perhaps it is simplistic of me to continue to draw on the analogy of the love we human parents have for our offspring, but the parent–child bond illuminates our understanding of God better than anything else, and it has the authority of Christ himself behind it. We who are fathers and mothers take joy in the life we're privileged to share with our children. We enjoy them when they're little and can't walk without holding our hands; we feel honored by the special things they share with us in trust during the tumultuous teenage years; and as we grow older, we delight in their adult companionship and the opportunities we have for mature dialogue. The theme of the sacred story in the Bible is that we are called into being to share life with God as his children forever.

---

12. Hanson, *Attractiveness*, 8 (italics added).
13. Ibid., 145 (italics added).

For Your Reflection

After reading chapter 3, "Experiencing God's Love"

- Have you ever felt *unconditional* love from another person? Who? When you were a child, who made you feel the most loved? What did this person do to make you feel that way?

- How did you think about God when you were a small child? How did you think about God when you were a teenager? How did you think about God before reading this chapter? Do you think differently about God now?

- Using your own words, how would you describe the relationship between Jesus and God? (Don't worry about trying to get the theological language just right; express your thoughts in your own words.)

- What do you think Jesus meant when he said, "Whoever does not receive the kingdom of God like a child shall not enter it" (Mark 10:15)?

- Is there an obstacle that makes it difficult for you to think of God as your loving "*Abba*"? What is it? What do you think might help you get over it?

- What are the qualities you once possessed as a child that you think you need to rediscover in order to put yourself in the right relationship with God? Make a list of practical ways you, as an adult, can recover this kind of childlikeness.

Chapter 4

Responding to God's Love: Worship

[Jesus says], "The hour is coming, and now is, when the true worshipers will worship the Father in spirit and truth, for such the Father seeks to worship him. God is spirit, and those who worship him must worship in spirit and truth."

—JOHN 4:23–24

MORE OFTEN THAN NOT, when people who've been away from the church for a long time decide to give Christianity another try, the first thing they do is pick a church and attend a Sunday service. It might be the congregation to which they once belonged or a different congregation of the same denomination, or it might be the church of friends who invite the returnee to come to a service with them. It might even be an impulsive decision to turn into the parking lot of the first church they see while driving down the road. Whatever the circumstances, attending a Sunday service is usually the first step a returnee takes. Therefore, it's important for us to think seriously about worship: what it means and where it fits in the Christian way of life.

People who were brought up as Christians but absent themselves from the church for a period of years leave for different reasons, and they return for different reasons. They have more motives than I can list, but here are a few I've observed as a pastor.

- Some young adults return to their faith because they marry and have children and want their children to share the same formative experience mom and dad had. The parents reason, "Growing up in the church was good for us, and it will be good for our children."

- Others return because they've experienced a deeply moving existential crisis that launched them on a quest to find a new meaning for their life.

- Still others come back to church because they've grown aware of a "God-shaped hole" in their souls and want to satisfy an instinctive hunger for God.

- Some are simply looking for community, for friends with whom they can join in meaningful service to others and share the joys and sorrows of life.

- Lastly, there are people who have experienced what felt like God's touch on their lives—perhaps a seemingly miraculous escape without injury from a car wreck where others died, a mystical moment of inspiration on a mountain top, or reading a verse from the Bible, quoted in a novel, that suddenly "spoke" to them.

People often choose to begin their return to Christian faith with a visit to a Sunday service, and they do so for many reasons. But in this chapter, I want to make the case for why people who have chosen to return to the practice of Christian faith and follow Jesus as their guide—as well as those who want to restart their journey—should choose to make worship, both public and private, a continuing key ingredient in their way of life.

The first reason we decide to commit ourselves to worship God is simply that we recognize it as our duty: it's what we *owe* God. Quoting the Tudor English of Thomas Cranmer, in its traditional Eucharistic rite, the Book of Common Prayer of the Episcopal Church says, "It is very meet, right, and our bounden duty, that we should at all times and in all places, give thanks unto thee, O Lord, holy Father, almighty, everlasting God."[1] There's nothing wrong with duty; many of the best things we do in life are done out of a sense of duty. And I know from personal experience that many of us who try to follow Jesus with great dedication often participate in formal worship for many years mainly out of duty, until the liberating grace of God's great love finally breaks through and floods our hearts. Maybe that's truer for people like me who were raised in pious households where God seemed more like a Lawgiver than it is for those who were taught from childhood to think of God as a patient and loving Father. But even for those of us who grew up with a Critical Parent picture of God, the longer we faithfully walk in the footsteps of Jesus, the more likely we are to discover

---

1. Book of Common Prayer, The Holy Eucharist: Rite One, Eucharistic Prayer One, 333.

Responding to God's Love: Worship

that we're not just worshiping out of duty but out of *joy* and a *desire* to worship—because we feel God's love, and worship is one of the main ways we can love God back.

It's a gift to be loved. Unless our emotions have been crippled by hate, the experience of being loved evokes love from us in return. When anyone gives us a gift, even if it's our birthday and we're more or less expecting gifts, we normally express gratitude to the giver and typically look for an opportunity to reciprocate. I think this also holds true when we realize we're loved by God.

The New Testament says, "We love, because [God] first loved us" (1 John 4:19). But the apostle didn't write "We love *God* because he first loved us." He's telling his readers that we have any love at all to give—whether to God or our spouses or our children or our neighbors—only because God has loved us first. God's gift of love enables us to love. But to be empowered by the gift of divine love, we—metaphorically speaking—have to open that gift and use it. We need to untie the bow, take off the gift wrapping, remove the lid, and "put on" our *Abba's* love the way we'd put on a new, warm sweater on Christmas morning.

God's love, just like any other gift we're offered, can be declined, ignored, or hidden on a closet shelf to be opened later, if at all. Some sincere disciples of Jesus take a long time before they're ready and able to open that gift, but eventually they will. God's love is the most powerful force in the universe.

When asked to name the greatest commandment in the law, Jesus famously said, "'You shall love the Lord your God with all your heart, and with all your soul, and with all your mind.' This is the great and first commandment. And a second is like it, 'You shall love your neighbor as yourself.' On these two commandments depend all the law and the prophets" (Matt 22:37–40, quoting Deut 6:5 and Lev 19:18).

We can obey the two great commandments Jesus named only because we've been empowered by the love God has given us. Loving God and loving our fellow human beings are both *responses* to the experience of being loved by God. When we're moved to show our love to God, I believe the shape our love most perfectly takes is *worship*, and I mean worship in many different forms. That includes worship together with the people of God (what we typically do on Sundays), but it also includes the private expressions of worship that we articulate for ourselves and that grow to have deep meaning for us. As we make our journey with Jesus, attentive to what we're taught about him in the gospels, we see that his whole life, day by day, was an obedient, joyful, prayer-filled, worshipful response to the experience of his Father's love.

I've been an Episcopal priest since 1972, but until I went to college I was a Presbyterian, and as was true back in the 1950s for all good Presbyterian children, when I became twelve years old, our pastor expected me to memorize the Westminster Shorter Catechism, a document written in the mid-seventeenth century by a diverse assembly of theologians chosen by Parliament to bring a thoroughgoing Calvinistic reformation to the Church of England. Our pastor gave me a little booklet with the catechism in it, and I proceeded to learn it. I'll never forget the first question it asked: "What is the chief end of man?" And the answer: "Man's chief end is *to glorify God, and enjoy him forever.*"[2] When I was twelve I wondered how anybody could possibly "enjoy" God, especially forever. Sitting still in church every Sunday during a forty-five-minute sermon felt like forever to a squirmy seventh grader, and I was always glad for the Sundays when my mother let me sit in the last pew with an older boy so we could play tic-tac-toe during the sermon.

I still wonder about that old catechism's first question and answer, but now they strike me as profound: "Man's chief end is to glorify God, and enjoy him forever." If we haven't yet discovered how to *enjoy* God, what does it take to get started? I don't think we can really begin fully enjoying God until we finally realize that we're God's own children and he truly delights in us. Becoming aware of God's love is the key. Once that happens, we worship God in private and gather with others to worship God in public simply because we "enjoy God."

A number of passages in the Bible are efforts to draw pictures with words in order to open a window into heaven, where it seems the main activity is *worship*. But it's not worship as seen from the perspective of a twelve-year-old who'd rather play tic-tac-toe. It's worship that's totally engaging. If we follow hints we find in the Psalms, it appears that biblical worship includes many truly pleasurable activities: not only harp playing (traditionally associated with heaven, at least by cartoonists), but also organ playing, trumpet playing, bell ringing, cymbal clanging, drum beating, hand clapping, singing, dancing, and even shouting. Doesn't all that

2. Williamson, *Westminster*, 1.

hullabaloo sound like fun? Such joyful, godly activities may be what the solemn theologians who met at Westminster Abbey back in 1647 had in mind when they wrote that man's chief end is to glorify God, and enjoy him forever.

The Psalms' picture of heavenly worship with harps, trumpets, cymbals, and drums reminds me of kindergarten, when the music teacher would hand out rattles, cricket clickers, jingle-bells, and tambourines and turn our class into a rhythm band. We were too young to be self-conscious and perfectionistic. We were totally spontaneous preschoolers, and so we just made a lot of noise—with precious little rhythm—but we were happy and had a great time. Rhythm band was the high point of our kindergarten day. Never forget: Jesus says we have to become like little children to enter the kingdom of God.

When John the Seer, who wrote the book of Revelation, describes his dreams of heaven, they feature vast scenes of praise and adoration being offered by angels, archangels, cherubim, seraphim, and the assembly of the redeemed, gathered before the throne of God and the Lamb. Therefore, since we're Christians who believe heaven is our destiny—accessible to us right now, not only in a distant *postmortem* future—we have to believe that our destiny is to glorify God and enjoy him forever. The glorifying and enjoying starts as we begin to return our *Abba's* love.

I propose a definition of worship. Our word *worship* is a contraction of an early English word we would spell as *worth-ship*, and it is the human activity that acknowledges the supreme worth, value, dignity, and status of God in comparison with everything else. It's by worshiping God that we demonstrate how important God is to us. Participation in public worship proclaims to the world that God is our highest good—number one in our lives. And the practice of worshiping while alone—what one might call private worship—reinforces and renews that conviction in our own minds day by day.

In the book of Revelation, at the very end of the Bible, are some short hymns we still hear in churches. Two of the best known are familiar from their use in Handel's *Messiah*, "Hallelujah, for the Lord our God the Almighty reigns" and "Worthy is the Lamb that was slain to receive power and riches and wisdom and might and honor and glory and blessing" (Rev 19:6; 5:12). We can place with those the twenty-four elders' song of praise

Finding the Way

as they prostrate themselves before the heavenly throne and chant, "You are worthy, O Lord our God, to receive glory and honor and power; for you have created all things and by your will they were created and have their being" (Rev 4:11). These hymns from the Bible affirm the "worthiness" of God and his rightful place as recipient of our reverence and worship: *Worthy is the Lamb! O Lord our God, you are worthy!*

A social scientist wanting to write a formal description of Christian religious acts might call our worship "normatizing valuing behavior"—a mouthful of words meaning "actions that reinforce our personal value system"—with the top rank, the ultimate value, belonging to God, and everything else being ranked as of lower value to us than God. This is what people must mean when they tell us, "God comes first in my life, and then my family, and then my work."

But this is only true when our acts of religious worship are authentic and sincere. We'd have to admit that if something other than God is really taking over the number one place in our day-to-day valuing behavior, even if we are also attending church on Sundays and participating in pubic worship, then whatever has in actual practice been given the place of highest value in our lives has become *de facto* a rival god, an *idol*. Anything that receives the lion's share of our time, imagination, intellect, money, energy, and passion has become our god, the real object of our worship, even if we deny that our valuing behavior is technically "worship" at all. If the focus of our ordinary valuing behavior (meaning the investment of our total available personal resources, tangible and intangible) is other than God, we're engaging in idolatry. We're worshiping something that lacks ultimate worth, sacrificing to a false god—maybe even a whole pantheon of false gods—though they're not the kind who have statues or temples, like the gods and goddesses that were worshiped in ancient Babylon. The real test of whether or not our worship of God is authentic is the extent to which we give ourselves to worshiping while alone (what we might even call "secret worship"), as well as joining with others in public worship. I will say more about that at the end of this chapter.

Understanding all this should make it obvious that *worship* is a very important human activity. The word itself implies more than most people generally think. English bishop Tom Wright says, in his 2006 book *Simply Christian*, "You become like what you worship." What we worship shapes the person we are becoming, and it's true to say that everyone will, in time, worship something—even people who profess to be atheists—because, simply stated, our god is whatever we prize as most worthy. Here's what Bishop Wright wrote concerning what he called "two golden rules at the heart of spirituality," the first of which is the bit of wisdom I just quoted:

> *You become like what you worship.* When you gaze in awe, admiration, and wonder at something or someone, you begin to take on something of the character of the object of your worship. Those who worship money become, eventually, human calculating machines. Those who worship sex become obsessed with their own attractiveness or prowess. Those who worship power become more and more ruthless.
>
> So what happens when you worship the creator God whose plan to rescue the world and put it to rights has been accomplished by the Lamb who was slain? The answer comes in the second golden rule: because you were made in God's image, *worship makes you more truly human.* When you gaze in love and gratitude at the God in whose image you were made, you do indeed grow. You discover more of what it means to be fully alive.[3]

As we ponder the role of worship in our lives, there's another definition to consider, the meaning of *sacrifice*. I define it this way: *a sacrifice is a costly gift, joyfully given.* Social anthropologists and scholars in the field of religion tell us worship always involves sacrifice—the glad giving of a precious gift—because sacrifice is the only act that certifies the value that belongs to the object of my worship (i.e., my god). If I say, "I love the Lord my God with all my heart and soul and mind and strength," yet offer God nothing of real value to me—such as my time, imagination, intellect, money, energy, or passion—then my claim to love God is invalidated, and I'm revealed as a fraud. My behavior gives the lie to what I say and my behavior demonstrates that my *real* value-focus lies elsewhere, not with God, no matter how I may spend one hour every Sunday morning. When my most precious offerings, my most significant self-investments, are given to something else—such as improving my appearance, building my business, accumulating wealth, acquiring power over other people, seeking sensate pleasure, spending time on social networking websites, or even enhancing my education or acquiring a useful skill—then that "something else" is my idol, my false god. And when I worship my idol, that worship, little by little, shapes my life, my behavior, and my character.

---

3. Wright, *Simply Christian*, 148 (italics in original).

Finding the Way

Worship is always something we *do*. It's not a state of mind or a way we feel—whether we're speaking of worship offered by each of us in solitude or corporate, liturgical worship offered by a congregation. Corporate worship calls for mental and physical engagement, effort, and concentration, just as solitary worship does. In America today, our attitudes toward most things have been formed by years of being passive spectators—mainly sitting in front of television sets, seeking entertainment or escape. This tends to make us treat worship services in church as commodities, "performances" provided to inspire, educate, improve, or entertain us.

We're predisposed to think of *ourselves* as the focus of public worship, and so we tend to behave as passive consumers of "spiritual goods and services" rather than as dynamic participants in a life-enhancing activity—worship of the all-holy God. Our social orientation as consumers drives us to think of what goes on in church on Sunday morning as something aimed at us, done for us, designed to bless us or help us or teach us or make us better people. But that's not really what worship is all about! Authentic worship with a community is always *participatory*, not passive, *and it's about God, not us.*

It's possible there might be uplifting music, inspiring preaching, and splendid ceremony during a Sunday liturgy in the church of our choice. It's possible that those services are almost always aesthetically pleasing. We hope they are. But it's also possible—perhaps even likely—that they're usually *not*. In the churches where most of us worship on a typical Sunday, the hymns might often be quaint and out of date and the musicians amateurs, the preacher might be ill-prepared and difficult to hear, and the ceremony itself disorganized and bumbling. Its aesthetic quality as judged by a church critic writing a worship review column (if there were such a thing) might be given "one-half star out of a possible four." But that need have no effect on our ability to worship God, *because the authenticity of our worship is based on what we intend*, on what we bring to the occasion, not the skills of the ministers and musicians or what we might later decide we got out of it.

Whether or not the music or the preaching or the ceremony is inspiring, the congregation isn't there to be an audience, prepared either to applaud or hiss, depending on the quality of the "performance." The people of the congregation are gathered to make an offering of themselves, their souls and bodies, "as a reasonable, holy and living sacrifice" to God.[4] Whatever

---

4. See Rom 12:1; See also the Book of Common Prayer, 336.

inspiration, education, or information worshipers derive from the occasion is simply a desirable by-product of the enterprise, not its main purpose.

I don't want to imply that there's not supposed to be helpful content for worshipers in the liturgies celebrated in our respective churches on Sunday morning. As a pastor, I want people to be affected in a positive way by every service. The readings from Scripture are meant to convey the Word of God. The sermon is meant to expound that Word and call us to respond. The sharing of Holy Communion is intended to unite us in a mystical way with Christ in his self offering and link us to one another. The prayers and hymns are supposed to be vehicles for the expression of our love for God. Worship in Word and Sacrament is—as we were taught in confirmation classes—a "means of grace." But, if none of the elements of worship works for us, or pleases us, and if we don't get anything out of the service, that need not keep us from worshiping God—not if our hearts are in the right place, not if we keep our loving focus on God rather than ourselves.

Liturgy actually means "public service" or "the work of the people," and that definition of public worship applies just as well for Baptists or Pentecostals, who use no fixed forms in their services, as it does for Catholics, Episcopalians, or Lutherans, whose services are dictated by an established ritual. In every case, worship demands that participants be focused, engaged, and active in the process of making an offering of themselves to God. But that's easier said than done.

Lutheran New Testament professor Mark Allan Powell writes in his book, *Loving Jesus*, about beginning his ordained ministry as the young assistant pastor of a church whose senior pastor assigned him the unenviable task of making home visits to people who had stopped attending services. When he went to call on those dropouts, he heard many different reasons for why they had stopped coming to church. But most of the reasons boiled down to, "I quit coming to church because I wasn't getting out of it what I thought I should get out of it." Mark Powell writes,

> This struck me as odd. When I was little, my mother used to pile us in the car every Sunday morning and drive us to church, and she would say, "We are going to worship God." I always thought *that* was why people went to church: to worship God. But these inactive members, apparently, did not have mothers like mine, and they had all somehow gotten the idea that the *reason* one goes to church is to get something out of it. Frankly, as a child I'm not sure if I ever expected to get anything out of it or not. At any rate, that

wasn't the point. "Six days a week, God is good to us," my mother would say, "and on Sundays we give thanks."[5]

Powell asserts that Christians gather to worship God simply *because God is worthy of our worship.* He adds, "That will not change. No one so far has ever told me, 'Well, pastor, I quit coming to church because I decided that God just isn't really *worthy* of being worshiped any more.'"[6]

Worship is about God, and God *deserves* to be worshiped. It's an offering whereby we confess and reaffirm the worth of God and his importance to us. Americans revere "the market," and the market says we demonstrate the relative value of a thing by how much we're willing to pay for it. Observation of ordinary life demonstrates that we invest ourselves deeply only in things that truly matter to us. If education matters to us, then when we're in school we study. If a sport matters to us, we practice so we can play it well. If our financial investments matter to us, we manage those investments carefully. And if God matters to us, if we've been touched and given life by God's love, *then we will be serious about worship because we're serious about God.* God matters.

We work at what matters to us, and worship calls us to work, both when the worship leaders are skilled and when they're not. It's a sacrificial offering of our minds, imaginations, and energy to God. There's a paradox in worship, though, and please don't miss it. God is the focus and recipient of our worship, *but the truth is that worship really only benefits us.* After all, God doesn't need our praises, our offerings, or our attention. God has no needs, no deficiencies. God isn't like an insecure human being who will be unable to function unless he gets plenty of affirmation from us so he feels important. But the truth is that our souls will wither and die if we *don't* worship. Worship, however, only benefits us when we are mentally, physically, and spiritually engaged in that holy work.

Worship, ideally, is a self-emptying experience, an *ecstatic* experience, keeping in mind that the meaning of the Greek word *ekstasis* is "to be beside oneself, amazed, or astonished." Self-emptying can never happen if, in worship, we're always taking our spiritual temperature and asking, "Am I getting anything out of this?" When our attention is focused on ourselves and the quest for satisfaction of our perceived needs, we can't worship at all. But if we're able to stand outside ourselves, empty ourselves of self-regard, and pour out our worship in love for God, we will be blessed. The same

5. Powell, *Loving Jesus*, 130–31 (italics in original).
6. Ibid., 131 (italics added).

Responding to God's Love: Worship

spiritual principle is at work in worship that Jesus expressed when he said, "He who loses his life for my sake will find it" (Matt 10:39).

Worship is similar to the experience of giving a beautiful gift to the person we love the most. If we're in love, we want to give precious gifts and do wonderful things for our beloved. The cash or personal effort that might be required is no obstacle. The love we feel inspires us to sacrifice, and a sacrifice is "a costly gift *joyfully* given." That is to say, the genuine offering of a sacrifice never leaves us feeling deprived. The opposite is the case. Our sacrifice produces in us a sense of deeply gratifying joy. A medieval mystic once said about Jesus' self-offering that it was our Savior's *joy* to give his life on the cross for us. John's gospel (12:1–8) tells about Mary of Bethany pouring a huge quantity of precious ointment over Jesus' feet, then wiping them with her hair. The story says the only person who objected to such extravagance was Judas Iscariot.

Those who love God with all their heart and soul and mind and strength are going to be happy to sacrifice their time, imagination, intellect, money, energy, and passion on him. Our songs of praise, our prayers in public and when alone, and our personal gestures of devotion—even ones as simple as making it a practice to send little "arrow prayers" to God all through the day, or coming into church ten minutes before the liturgy begins and kneeling in total silence before God for those minutes—are our own costly perfume poured out on the Lord's feet because we love him.

In the Sermon on the Mount, Jesus says, "When you pray, you must not be like the hypocrites; for they love to stand and pray in the synagogues and at the street corners, that they may be seen by men. Truly, I say to you, they have received their reward. But when you pray, go into your room and shut the door and pray to your Father who is in secret; and your Father who sees in secret will reward you" (Matt 6:5–6).

We know that Jesus had no objection to worshiping in the synagogue, joining with others to offer the psalms and prayers that composed the Jewish liturgy of his time. He participated in synagogue services regularly, and even the Pharisees could find nothing to criticize about Jesus' proper Jewish piety. But Jesus found fault with the ostentatious practices of certain Pharisees who paraded their personal devotions in public, either in a synagogue or on the street, in order to impress other people with their holiness. Synagogues were places of study as well as worship. A man who came into the synagogue other than at the usual hours of daily prayer, put on his *tallit* (prayer shawl) and *tefillin* (phylacteries), and offered audible

63

vocal prayer while others were quietly studying or discussing Torah would definitely draw attention to himself.

Jesus encouraged his disciples to offer their solitary prayers in a "secret place," which simply meant a place away from the eyes and ears of others. Jesus regularly left his friends and went away by himself to pray (Matt 14:23; Mark 1:35; Luke 5:16), though there were also times—other than during synagogue worship—when he prayed in their presence, as on the Mount of Transfiguration and in the Garden of Gethsemane (Mark 14:31–42; Luke 9:21–36; 11:1–4). Prayer in solitude, which we might label "private worship," is as important as the public worship we offer with other Christians in church on Sundays. In some ways, solitary worship, our "secret prayer," is even more important, since our practice of prayer in private is intensely personal, hidden from the view of others, and—at least potentially—able to express the most sincere thoughts and feelings of our hearts. Its form is not dictated by the church, and no observers are present to criticize how we choose to pray. It's an activity known to God alone, and the "sacrifice of prayer" we offer then may take whatever shape is most meaningful to us. Those who neglect worship in solitude can scarcely make a case that they love God very much, to say nothing of loving God with all their heart and soul and mind and strength.

There is a void in the human heart, and every person alive is trying to fill it with something. There's an empty shrine at the center of our souls, the place that was made for God to dwell, because God made us for himself. Worship opens the door and lets him in.

Responding to God's Love: Worship

∽ ∽ ∽

For Your Reflection

After reading chapter 4, "Responding to God's Love: Worship"

- Why do you go to church on Sunday?
- Has this chapter reshaped your thinking about worship? What has changed?
- Can you think of someone you loved so much as a child or teenager that you wanted always to please that person and never disappoint him or her? (I am not referring to romantic attachments.) What made you feel that way toward this person?
- Keeping in mind the point that *worship* is the activity that identifies what one values the most, when you look at how you have invested your own time, imagination, intellect, money, energy, and passion thus far in life, would you say that you have ever worshiped any *idols*? What have been those idols?
- Bishop Tom Wright said, "You become like what you worship." Does that feel true to you? Why or why not?
- A medieval saint said that it was our Savior's joy to give his life on the cross for us. How does that shape your understanding of joy? What experiences have given you that kind of joy?
- Worship in solitude is just as important as public worship. If you have never had a rule of regular personal private prayer ("secret" prayer, as described in this chapter), try adopting such a discipline now. Don't measure the amount of time you spend in prayer, simply pray regularly for as long as feels right.
- Here are a few "arrow prayers" you can offer silently while you're doing other things, such as driving the car, shoveling snow, changing a baby's diaper, preparing supper, or riding your bicycle. Choose one and repeat it slowly in your mind over and over. Don't quickly jump from one arrow prayer to another. Compose some arrow prayers of your own. You can teach these short, simple prayers to children.
    - "Lord Jesus Christ, Son of God, have mercy on me, a sinner." (This is the ancient "Jesus Prayer." You may shorten it

Finding the Way

if you wish. Note that to ask for mercy simply means to ask God to meet your needs, and God knows what those needs are. You don't have to tell him.)

- "Father, I adore you, lay my life before you. How I love you!"
- "This is my Father's world."
- "Lord, thank you for being with me right now."
- "Jesus loves me!"
- "Thank you, Lord, for this precious moment."
- "Your grace is sufficient for me."
- "Your will be done."

Chapter 5

Responding to God's Love: Prayer

[Jesus says], "When you pray, you must not be like the hypocrites; for they love to stand and pray in the synagogues and at the street corners, that they may be seen by men. Truly, I say to you, they have received their reward. But when you pray, go into your room and shut the door and pray to your Father who is in secret; and your Father who sees in secret will reward you.

And in praying do not heap up empty phrases as the Gentiles do; for they think that they will be heard for their many words. Do not be like them, for your Father knows what you need before you ask him. Pray then like this: Our Father who art in heaven, Hallowed be thy name. Thy kingdom come. Thy will be done, On earth as it is in heaven. Give us this day our daily bread; And forgive us our debts, As we also have forgiven our debtors; And lead us not into temptation, But deliver us from evil."

—MATTHEW 6:5-13

PRAYER IS ANY DELIBERATE *activity meant to turn us toward God.* That's an intentionally broad definition because I want to offer a correction to the more restricted, formal understanding of prayer many of us learned from our parents or Sunday School teachers, which identified prayer as "talking to God," preferably with bowed heads, folded hands, and bended knees. That might describe the way we still pray in church during Sunday worship and, as I have already explained, all prayer *is* worship. But talking to God on bended knee is only a single "genus" within the large "family" of spiritual activities we call *prayer*. Our private prayers should actively disclose the meditations and intentions of our hearts to God—even though we recognize that God, "to whom all hearts are open, all desires known, and from whom no secrets are hid,"[1] can read our hearts quite well without help from us. I will say more about this later, but if prayer is understood as any deliberate activity meant to turn us toward God, then prayer must include *everything we choose to do*—every posture we assume and every place we go—as well as everything we say or think about with the purpose of orienting our souls to God.

Why would people want to orient themselves to God? The only answer I can offer is very simple: People want to orient themselves to God because they find God incredibly attractive. I do, and I know many others who feel the same way. For us, God is "magnetic." We feel an inward hunger for God, a need for God, a desire for God. We are more interested in having a close relationship with God than in anything else.

I believe many people feel this attraction to one degree or another, including some who are not outwardly religious in the conventional sense. I read in the *New York Times* last year that, according to a poll of young adults eighteen to twenty-nine years of age (the Millennial Generation), "being spiritual or close to God" was the most selected "primary long-term life goal." Other choices those polled could have marked included "to get married and have a family" and "to get rich." The rate at which this age cohort selected "being spiritual or close to God" was significantly higher than all other generational groups, and nearly twice that of Gen X (those born between 1965 and 1981).[2]

This tells us there are people who are not conventionally religious but would like to have a relationship with God. They feel the attractiveness of God. At the same time, we know there are people who attend church or synagogue and recite ritual prayers, but are not intentionally *oriented* to God. Such people may be participating in religious rituals because they have been culturally conditioned to do so. For example, some Jews do not believe in God but *do* believe in the religious traditions of Judaism as the essential glue of their culture. There are cultural Christians, too, who don't believe in God, but *do* believe in religion. There are also people who say formal prayers because they're superstitious, although they would not choose to describe

---

1. From the Collect for Purity, which is placed near the beginning of the Eucharist in most Anglican rites. Thomas Cranmer translated the prayer into English from the Latin of the Sarum Missal for the 1549 Book of Common Prayer, and from there it has entered almost every Anglican prayer book in the world.

2. Blow, "Spirit Quest," n.p.

themselves that way. They're afraid something bad might happen to them if they don't keep going through the motions of religious observance.

I believe those who have a deep desire to pray do so because, in a psychological sense, they cannot *not* pray. God is drawing them to himself with a magnetic intensity that feels almost as strong as the physical need for air, food, water, or sleep. And that deep sense of need never completely goes away. This is what writers on Christian spirituality since the earliest centuries have called our natural "hunger for God."

Those familiar with the hierarchy of needs articulated back in the mid-1940s by the humanistic psychologist Abraham Maslow might say that the felt hunger for a relationship with God—the ground out of which our need to pray grows—is not really like the *physiological* need for air, food, water and sleep to which I just compared it, but instead is more like the capstone of Maslow's needs pyramid, the need for what he labeled self-actualization.

After all, we can have too much food; we can grow obese. We can have too much water; we can poison our systems by drinking too much of it. But, unlike physiological needs, the need for self-actualization can never be fully satisfied. We can never have too much. By the same token, the need for God can never be fully satisfied either, at least not in this life. We can never have too much of a relationship with God in the same way that we might sometimes have too much food or water or sleep. If we have a healthy respiratory system, however, we can never have too much air. (It's interesting that the biblical words for *spirit* and *air* are the same.)

According to Maslow's theory, as the human person grows psychologically and spiritually there are always fresh opportunities to keep growing. In Maslow's psychology, self-actualized people are motivated by the quest for Truth, Justice, Wisdom, or Meaning, and none of these can ever be fully comprehended by us. There is more to each of them than our finite intelligence can grasp. Although Abraham Maslow rejected organized religion, he appears not to have cut himself off from his Jewish roots, because—as Jewish and Christian teachers alike have always taught—we can never exhaust all the possibilities in a relationship with God and, therefore, we can never deplete all the potential in prayer. To pray is to "seek the face of God" as Psalm 27 describes it.[3] We indeed "seek God's face," but the Bible also

---

3. "You speak in my heart and say, 'Seek my face.' Your face, Lord, will I seek. Hide not your face from me, nor turn away your servant in displeasure" (Ps 27:11–12).

tells us we cannot see the face of God and live. We can only see God as he chooses to reveal himself, and we Christians believe that God reveals himself in the face of Jesus.

I believe that those who are drawn to pray and worship do so because deep within our souls we feel God pulling us to himself the way a magnet attracts iron. Having felt that way, we still might turn away from God for a season or sometimes even years—perhaps out of anger at the church, spite towards domineering parents, or disappointment that our earnest prayers did not lead to a miraculous recovery from cancer for someone we loved. But such temporarily alienated individuals often ultimately turn back to God, because God is always drawing them to himself with an almost irresistible force.

It's useful to learn from the examples of prayer we find in the Bible. We can go all the way back to Genesis and see how the patriarchs spoke with God. The dialogues between Abraham and God or between Moses and God are not foreign to our own way of praying. Indeed, the intimacy—we might even call it familiarity—apparent in the Hebrew patriarchs' prayers shows that the idea of personal closeness between God and his children has Old Testament roots. An obvious example is the conversation between Abraham and the Lord in Genesis 18, after God has announced his plan to destroy the wicked city of Sodom, where Abraham's nephew Lot had taken up residence. Here is that divine–human interaction as paraphrased by Eugene Peterson in *The Message*:

> Abraham confronted [God], "Are you serious? Are you planning on getting rid of the good people right along with the bad? What if there are fifty decent people left in the city; will you lump the good with the bad and get rid of the lot? Wouldn't you spare the city for the sake of those fifty innocents? I can't believe you'd do that, kill off the good and the bad alike as if there were no difference between them. Doesn't the Judge of all the Earth judge with justice?"
>
> God said, "If I find fifty decent people in the city of Sodom, I'll spare the place just for them."
>
> Abraham came back, "Do I, a mere mortal made from a handful of dirt, dare open my mouth again to my Master? What if the fifty fall short by five—would you destroy the city because of those missing five?"

He said, "I won't destroy it if there are forty-five."
Abraham spoke up again, "What if you only find forty?"
"Neither will I destroy it if for forty."
He said, "Master, don't be irritated with me, but what if only thirty are found?"
"No, I won't do it if I find thirty."
He pushed on, "I know I'm trying your patience, Master, but how about for twenty?"
"I won't destroy it for twenty."
He wouldn't quit, "Don't get angry, Master—this is the last time. What if you only come up with ten?"
"For the sake of only ten, I won't destroy the city." When God finished talking with Abraham, he left. And Abraham went home (Gen 18:21–33 *The Message*.)

This scene makes us imagine a buyer and seller bargaining in a Near Eastern bazaar, and no doubt that was the author's intent. But the significant thing about it is its portrayal of the freedom of speech to which the children of God are entitled, the privilege of speaking their minds to the Father. It might not immediately strike us as being *prayer*, but it is an illustration of Abraham and God talking together about something very important. That makes it prayer.

Because our journey as disciples of Jesus is meant to be an imitation of Christ, it's logical for us to want to pray as Jesus prayed. After all, that's what it means to pray "in Jesus' name," as he taught us. "In Jesus' name" is not merely a formal way to conclude our prayers. It means we are seeking to pray as Jesus prayed—indeed, seeking to pray *as if we were Jesus*—standing in the same relationship of intimacy with the Father, intending as he did to abide in the center of our Father's will. To learn about Jesus' prayers, we turn to the gospels. They tell us that Jesus sometimes went off into the countryside and prayed alone, at least once rising before dawn and going out into the Galilean hills and another time spending a whole night in prayer before choosing the twelve men who would be his closest disciples.[4]

We have no idea exactly what those hours of solitary prayer were like. Was Jesus talking to God all the time, forming words, articulating requests, and hearing words in reply? Probably not. I imagine that for most of those long hours of prayer he was simply experiencing the closeness of his *Abba*,

---

4. See Mark 1:35; Luke 6:12.

wordless communion with God, much as we can experience intimacy with the people we love the most without actually doing much talking. (I'm a loquacious person, but my wife has taught me how people who love each other deeply can enjoy one another's presence without too much talking. Simply being together is often enough.)

The New Testament also portrays Jesus speaking directly to the Father in prayers that were audible to bystanders, as in John 12:27–28, where in the midst of a Jerusalem crowd he says, "Now is my soul troubled. And what shall I say? 'Father, save me from this hour'? No, for this purpose I have come to this hour. Father, glorify thy name." And the voice of God then speaks like thunder, saying, "I have glorified it, and I will glorify it again." Surely, there must have been many occasions when Jesus prayed aloud to his *Abba* without hearing an audible heavenly voice in reply, though he often heard the Father speaking, as we can, in the Scriptures.

Luke's gospel portrays the transfiguration as an occasion when Jesus invites Peter, James, and John—the inner circle of the Twelve—to accompany him on a trek up to a mountain top to pray. There they see him transfigured (literally, *metamorphosed*) and speaking with Elijah and Moses. Was Jesus' dialogue with these two great figures out of Israel's history meant to be understood as an aspect of prayer? Or was he transfigured by his prayer-filled reflection on the Law and the Prophets? However we understand the transfiguration, the story shows Jesus visibly and gloriously changed *by praying* (Luke 9:21–36).

Further on in Luke, after being in Jesus' company as again he was praying, the Twelve ask him to teach them how to pray. These Jewish men who have been praying all their lives know about conventional prayer; but they see something special, something different, in Jesus' prayer, and they want him to teach them how to pray as he prays. Did they hope to learn how to pray in a way that would result in their own transfiguration or permit them to have dialogue with great prophets? In response to his friends' request, Jesus tells them, "When you pray, say," and then he articulates what Protestants call the Lord's Prayer and other Christians call the Our Father (Luke 11:1–4). The version we find in Luke is shorter and simpler than the one in Matthew (6:1–14), hence it is thought by some to be closer to Jesus' original choice of words than Matthew's version. The prayer in Matthew seems to have been edited into a more formal, literary style, with a traditional Jewish doxology added at the end: "For thine is the kingdom and the power and the glory forever. Amen." The form most widely used in Christian worship is a blend of the two, and the traditional English version is still the most familiar to Americans: "Our Father, who art in heaven, hallowed be thy Name, thy kingdom come, thy will be done, on earth as it is in heaven. Give us this day our daily bread. And forgive us our trespasses, as we forgive those who trespass against us. And lead us not into temptation, but deliver us from evil. [For thine is the kingdom, and the power, and the glory forever. Amen.]"[5]

Before thinking about the Lord's Prayer as a model for our own prayer, it's worth noting that the early church regarded this prayer as a singular gift from Jesus to his disciples. It was not shared with those who had not been baptized. It was taught to new believers as part of their formal baptismal instruction, but they did not pray it until a point at the beginning of the baptism liturgy.[6]

The first thing we notice is that Jesus tells his friends to address their prayers simply to "our Father," without an elaborate salutation such as, "O, Almighty and everlasting God." The two little words "our Father" remind us that even if we're alone on a mountainside, we inevitably pray as members of a vast family, who rightly give our sisters' and brothers' needs the same attention we give our own. The petitions of Jesus' model prayer start with adoration—"Hallowed be thy name"—which asks that God's *name*, understood by Jews to mean God's *presence*, be regarded with reverence and holy dread. It's an awesome thing to be welcomed into the presence of God and invited to approach the Almighty with the intimacy and freedom of beloved children. Therefore, we do well to spend some time in silence before we offer our words to God, gathering our thoughts and recalling the glory of the One we're privileged to call our *Abba*.

Our Father never forces us to obey him. He shows us the path of life, but allows us to choose our own way forward. Therefore, to pray, "thy kingdom come, thy will be done on earth as it is in heaven," places our yearning for the fulfillment of God's purposes and our acknowledgment of his authority in human affairs—both of which require our cooperation—ahead of everything else we might seek. It aligns us with the central proclamation of Jesus' own ministry, "The kingdom of God is at hand" (Mark 1:15). The coming of God's kingdom and the doing of God's will are two ways of describing

---

5. The most commonly used form of the Lord's Prayer is the one found in Matthew, except for the petition, "And forgive us our debts, as we forgive our debtors," for which most denominations—except for churches in the Presbyterian and Reformed tradition—substitute language from the prayer as found in Luke, "forgive us our trespasses, as we forgive those who trespass against us."

6. See Theodore, "Commentary," 33.

the same thing. (Parallelism is a common rhetorical device in Hebrew.) To pray for God's will to " be done on earth as it is in heaven" is, indeed, to pray that earth *become* heaven, the realm where God's dominion is perfect. In this phase of our journey home to God, our daily prayers are necessarily filled with petitions about various concerns and needs that claim our attention, both for ourselves and for others. But the model prayer Jesus gives us provides in its opening petition the simple, final, and best summary of all possible petitions: that God's will, not ours, be done. This was Jesus' prayer in Gethsemane, and it is our own best possible prayer. We pray not in order to change God's mind, but to have the mind of Christ in ourselves.

Only after the great concerns for God's holiness and the coming of his kingdom have been named does Jesus tell his disciples to submit their own needs to the Father: "give us this day our daily bread." Recalling Jesus' reminder that we do not live "by bread alone, but by every word the proceeds from the mouth of God" (Matt 4:4), we may understand "daily bread" to mean both the material and the spiritual necessities of life, food for the body as well as food for the spirit.[7]

Next, we ask God to forgive our sins, with the qualifying condition that we also "forgive those who trespass against us." This petition recognizes that if we're unable freely to pardon others for their offenses against us, we have no claim on God's forgiveness for ourselves. If we use the form of the Our Father that imitates the version in Matthew, "forgive us our debts as we forgive our debtors," the words *debts* and *debtors* remind us that in God's eyes, our sins are not restricted to overtly evil acts, but also include our failures to behave as God has commanded. The second great commandment is "love your neighbor as yourself." Mercy and charity to others is a debt we owe God. Therefore, our failures to show compassion to others on occasions when we could have done so are as much in need of God's forgiveness as are our misdeeds.

One of our most frequent personal petitions to the Father is a plea for forgiveness. When we become aware of the numerous ways our choices pull us away from God and erect a barrier between us and the One who loves us, we are moved to cry out, "Lord, I am sorry! Have mercy on me and forgive me." Awareness of our sin and our need for God's mercy is a generator of prayer. Refusal to admit our own willingness to do evil is a refusal to accept

---

7. Matt 4:4, quoting Deut 8:3.

Responding to God's Love: Prayer

our own humanity. Michael Casey points out that we must get in touch with the truth of our own sinfulness before we can learn to pray.[8]

The exact meaning of the next-to-last petition of the Lord's model prayer might not seem very clear at first. Literally, "lead us not into temptation" (using a Greek word that also means *trials* or *testing*) could be understood as implying that God might sometimes cause temptations. But since the New Testament elsewhere tells us that God never tempts anyone to sin and that the temptations we face arise out of our own appetites and desires, I think it's unlikely that the earliest Christians ever understood this part of the Our Father as implying that God himself might tempt us to sin.[9] Matthew, Mark, and Luke agree that after Jesus had been baptized by his cousin John, the Holy Spirit led him into the wilderness to be tempted by Satan. Mark even says the Spirit "drove" Jesus out into the desert to encounter the devil.[10] Nowhere does the Bible say God "tempted" Jesus, but it does tell us that God put his Son in a position where he would be forced to confront temptation, and the Letter to the Hebrews later added that the Son of God "in every respect has been tempted as we are" (4:15).

God knows his children will be faced with temptations of various kinds during our lives. And we should understand that when those temptations come, they will always be, in some way, tests of our faith, character, or resolution to do the Father's will. That's what happens to Jesus in the Garden of Gethsemane, where he agonizes about accepting the terrible fate that is facing him: death at the hands of his enemies.

It's significant that when Jesus asks Peter, James, and John (the same men who were with him on the Mount of Transfiguration) to pray with him that night in Gethsemane, but later finds them sleeping, he tells them, "Watch and pray that you may not enter into temptation; the spirit indeed is willing, but the flesh is weak" (Matt 26:41). Jesus himself is struggling with temptation that very moment, temptation to avoid the cross. He knows from experience how terrible the struggle between flesh and spirit can be, and so he teaches his followers to ask, "lead us not into temptation." That's

---

8. Casey, *Toward God*, 150.

9. Jas 1:11–15: "Blessed is the man who endures trial, for when he has stood the test he will receive the crown of life which God has promised to those who love him. Let no one say when he is tempted, 'I am tempted by God'; for God cannot be tempted with evil and he himself tempts no one; but each person is tempted when he is lured and enticed by his own desire. Then desire when it has conceived gives birth to sin; and sin when it is full-grown brings forth death."

10. Matt 4:1; Mark 1:12; Luke 4:1.

a deeply human request, and a healthy one. Would any truly wise man or woman ever be eager for the moral struggle of serious temptation? Surely not. In light of that, Jesus links the two last petitions of his model prayer together with a conjunction, "lead us not into temptation, *but deliver us from evil.*" The gist of those connected petitions is: "Father, spare us the ordeal of testing; but if we must undergo such trials, keep us from falling into evil."

The Lord's model prayer demonstrates that if we want to pray as Jesus prayed, the heart of our prayer must be as his was: explicit trust in the Father. We put ourselves in God's hands. We express our confidence in God's provision. And we count on the Father to equip us to face whatever we must. It is true that meditation and wordless contemplative prayer are ancient Christian practices, but neither the saints of old nor those of today choose the prayer of silence to the *exclusion* of the kind of petitionary prayer we see modeled in our Lord's own prayer. Petition is the foundation of private prayer as well as of liturgical prayer, and for an important theological reason: it keeps us mindful of the *personhood* of God. Robert Llewelyn writes,

> *Once the concept of petition at the heart of prayer is surrendered, it will not be long before we relinquish the idea of God as personal*—and that is a statement which could equally well be put the other way round. The conceptions of God as Father and of prayer as petitionary are no more separable than the two sides of a coin. . . . Once we lose the concept of personality as applied to God it will not be long before we lose the concept of him as 'absolute demand' and so of ourselves as owing him 'total commitment'. That is probably the danger of what is called mystical religion when it is divorced from biblical theology.[11]

Those whose spirituality has been formed by the Bible use a personal pronoun (*he*) to speak of God, even though we know God has no gender, because the limits of language leave us the personal *he* as the only alternative to the impersonal *it*. The God who spoke to Abraham, Moses, and the Old Testament prophets, laying a claim on their lives, was intensely *personal*—definitely not an *it*. Jesus knew him and taught us to know him as *Abba*, our Father—not a vast, impersonal, diffused energy pervading the cosmos, whose power might be channeled by human reason for our own purposes, but rather a loving, accessible Person, whose heart is always open to his children. Llewelyn writes, "You can harness the power of steam

---

11. Llewelyn, "Prayer," 4 (italics added).

and use it for the propulsion of ships and trains, but you cannot address to steam the desires and aspirations of your heart."[12]

The only people who will engage in private, personal prayer are people of faith. Such prayer is *prima facie* evidence of faith. There are many reasons other than faith, however, that might lead some people to attend church on Sunday, such as to keep company with a devout spouse, to do the right thing for the children, to meet some nice people, to enjoy the music, or to admire the architecture. Private worship (personal prayer) is invariably motivated by some degree of faith, even when those who pray are harassed and distracted by unavoidable circumstances. It is the ordinary, day-by-day, week-in-week-out, confidential, intimate expression of love for God, our *Abba*.

This solitary prayer, this private worship that happens when we're out of sight and earshot of others, must assume whatever shape is most meaningful for each one of us. And that will vary from person to person. For example, a mother with young children might set her alarm to wake up before dawn most mornings, make a cup of coffee, then sit in a chair by a garden window with her cup and read a portion of Scripture, remaining there in silence afterwards, meditating on the words she read as sunlight floods into the garden. A businessman might close his office door after lunch most weekdays, push the "do not disturb" button on his phones, and spend the next half hour writing a letter to God in a journal, sometimes also writing what he imagines God might write back, if the Almighty were to reply to his letter. A college student might go out whenever she has free time and sit alone under a tree on the bank of a river, and—as she sits watching the river flow by, bearing leaves, branches and little ducks on its eddies—she relaxes her body, quiets her thoughts, and asks God to take her wherever he wants her to be, asking nothing more. A salesman with a very busy life—always on the go—might practice "crabgrass contemplation," a category of prayer-filled attentiveness that can flourish anywhere. Such contemplation demands the ability to notice and gaze in awe at the routine miracles of life, such as the crabgrass that can grow anywhere, even in a city parking lot, anyplace a crack in the asphalt offers a tiny space for a seed to germinate and grow.[13]

---

12. Llewelyn, Ibid., 5.
13. See Au, *Enduring*, 101–109. Chapter 6 is devoted to what the author calls "crabgrass contemplation."

Finding the Way

Our unique personal expression of love for God, our private prayers, will take many different forms during a lifetime, perhaps even during a single year. The way we pray as young parents will not be the way we pray as grandparents. What feels most authentic to us as new Christians is not likely to be a mode of praying that remains vital once we've been long mature in faith. Prayer does not always call for words on our part, either vocalized or mental; some of our most profound prayers are wordless. Mother Teresa of Calcutta was supposedly once asked by an interviewer, "When you pray, what you say to God?"

She replied, "I don't talk I listen."

The interviewer then asked, "What does God say to you?"

Mother Teresa answered, "He doesn't talk He listens."[14]

There's no single best way to pray, as long as our prayer rises from the heart. Maria Boulding was an English nun who lived her entire adult life in the cloister, yet never lost an innate awareness of what makes people tick. She writes about the ways our prayer can change with the seasons of life.

> *Prayer is not a hobby but a life, and to live is to change.* Human life is rhythmic: the body has its biological rhythms and its alternations between effort and rest, and on these are built the work-rhythms of our days and weeks. . . . Inevitably, prayer will be like this, too, since it is part of the plan of creation and redemption. You will know winter and spring, the disappointing gap when nothing seems to be happening between the glory of blossom-time and the appearance of the first tiny apples, and the deep peace of harvest. . . . Through the changes you must stick to prayer, regularly and hopefully, believing in the efficacious work that is going on in you.[15]

Prayer expresses a soul-deep yearning for union with God. It's not about achieving anything, though part of our prayer must always include the offering of our needs and desires to God—even if sometimes we're only asking for a deeper awareness of his presence. We have to avoid setting goals for ourselves in prayer, as we might do if we're preparing for a triathlon, or learning Spanish, or building a business. This also means steering

---

14. This story about Mother Teresa is apocryphal. It cannot be accurately documented, but it is repeated in many places online, with variations.

15. Boulding, *Prayer*, 75 (italics added).

clear of attempts to evaluate our prayer life, except to the extent that we're at some level aware of the long-term effects prayer is having on our life.

The *way* we pray matters less than *that* we pray. After all, personal, solitary prayer is about the intimate connection between each child of God and the Father. No one else is a party to the intimacy between God and us. It is uniquely sacred and deserves to be expressed in whatever form feels most authentic to the one who is praying. There is no competition; no judge will be observing our form and giving us marks for how we "perform" at prayer. If we choose to prostrate ourselves on the floor, that's fine. If we want to pray quietly while taking a walk, that's healthy for our body as well as our soul. If we want to stand with upraised arms, we may happily do so. If we want to be Pentecostal and pray in tongues, there's no problem. If we laugh or cry or shout, that also can be good—in the privacy of our own bedroom, on a riverbank, or anywhere we can be alone.

Because the two-thousand-year-long tradition of Christian prayer includes the widest possible variety of human beings, of different personality types and emotional and intellectual makeup, there can be no single, standard way of offering ourselves to God in prayer. There is more variety in methods of praying than anyone could possibly assimilate.[16] Therefore, the important thing is not to try out every possible prayer technique, but to find what works for us and stick with it—recognizing that sooner or later, in God's time, our usual way of praying will probably need to change. Kenneth Leech writes that we "learn to pray as we can and not as we cannot," but regardless of how we may choose to pray, our prayer should be contributing to our spiritual maturity and awareness of our true self.[17] If we feel that it's time to change our way of praying, then it probably is. If we're not sure, then we should ask for guidance from someone whose wisdom we trust.

The best analogy I can think of for a vibrant prayer life is being in love. When we're in love, our main goal in life is to spend as much time as possible in the company of our beloved. Five minutes on the phone listening to our sweetheart talk about anything that interests her or him is happier for us than an hour of serious conversation with a business colleague or joking with an old friend from college.

---

16. Entering *prayer techniques* into the Google search engine produced a list of more than twenty-seven million websites. Searching for *how to pray* on the Amazon website produced a list of over forty-one thousand books.

17. Leech, *True Prayer*, 27.

Finding the Way

Prayer is the fundamental act of faith. People who have many doubts and only a little faith will at least pray sometimes, but convinced atheists will not. Why should they? If a person is persuaded that there is no God, the sort of prayer I'm writing about would be absurd. But, then, not all prayer is Christian, and not all prayer is addressed to God.[18] A student of human behavior might say that prayer in itself is a natural activity for people, something all human beings do, whether they believe in a personal God or not. The "prayers" of those who acknowledge no god give voice to their wants and aspirations, and often their thankfulness, but are consciously addressed to nothing and no one except perhaps the cosmos in general or "the powers that be." All of us have heard friends who profess no belief in God say such things as, "I am so thankful you're all safe!" Who, precisely, are these people thanking? Our own prayers as followers of Christ are not categorically distinct from such basic human expressions of yearning, hope, or gratitude, but rather build on them and go beyond them.[19]

When in our solitude we seek the face of God, all that really matters is our *intent*, our honest desire to pray, whether we're praying aloud with only God to hear our voices, writing our prayers in a journal that won't be read by anyone else, meditating on a passage of Scripture chosen because it speaks God's wisdom to us, or sitting in contemplative silence, wordless and listening, lifting our emptiness to God. Thomas Merton believed that in the eyes of our loving Father, even though there may be times when we are so distracted, confused, or sick that we cannot pray, a simple, heartfelt *desire* to do so can count as prayer.

> Sometimes, meditation is nothing but an unsuccessful struggle to turn ourselves to God, to seek His Face by faith. Any number of things beyond our control may make it morally impossible for one to meditate effectively. In that case, faith and good will are sufficient. If one has made a really sincere and honest effort to turn himself to God and cannot seem to get his wits together at all, then the attempt will have to count as a meditation. This means that God, in His mercy, accepts our unsuccessful efforts in the place of a real meditation. Sometimes it happens that this interior helplessness is a sign of real progress in the interior

---

18. In the English of an earlier age, a "prayer" meant any sort of request. A Georgian lady might have said to a houseguest who was bidding her farewell, "Oh, friend, I pray you: stay with us another week." Formal legal language even in the United States still describes a petition to the law courts as a "prayer."

19. See Leech, *True Prayer*, 5–7.

life—for it makes us depend more completely and peacefully on the mercy of God.[20]

The purpose of prayer is to grow the relationship we have with God our *Abba* in union with Jesus, our brother and guide. Therefore, it's important for us to overcome the common temptation to think of prayer only in *functional* ways. We need to discard anxiety about the efficacy of our prayers or whether they are producing "results." Sometimes we have warm and positive—even exhilarated—feelings during or after prayer. But at other times we feel no emotions and even might imagine we've been wasting our time or that our prayer was unworthy. In times of depression or sadness, people can doubt whether God is listening or even cares. This variation of emotional response is normal, and Christians should not worry about the differences.

Christian prayer is not a technique for conjuring up warm, positive feelings. Just as a couple of glasses of wine may make a person feel quite cheerful, so might a happy hour of prayer. Or it might not. The quality or genuineness of our prayer does not depend on the emotions associated with it. Our feelings during prayer are irrelevant. We pray and we continue to pray out of our trust in God, perhaps even when we'd rather not be praying . . . perhaps even when it all seems foolish . . . perhaps even when our minds are riddled with doubts about God and ourselves. *But the very fact that we're praying at such times is a result of God's love at work deep within us.*

Michael Casey writes, "Our journey toward the Father is not made possible by anything we are or anything we do. It is entirely gift. By persevering in prayer one becomes strongly aware that prayer exceeds human capabilities. Much effort is involved in being faithful to prayer, but nothing we can do directly causes it to emerge."[21] Our relationship with God is not built from our side to his; instead, it starts with God seeking us. That's why some people say *prayer is received, not made.* The apostle Paul believed that the Spirit of God is at work in God's children to elicit from our hearts a kind of prayer that is often inarticulate, "too deep for words," but that nevertheless connects us with our *Abba*. He says, "the Spirit helps us in our weakness; for we do not know how to pray as we ought, but that very Spirit intercedes with sighs too deep for words. And God, who searches the heart, knows what is the mind of the Spirit, because the Spirit intercedes for the saints according to the will of God" (Rom 8:26–27).

---

20. Merton, *Thoughts*, 43.
21. Casey, *Toward God*, 148.

Finding the Way

It's difficult to know precisely what Paul meant by this, but it seems he saw so great a loving, caring connection between God and us that he conceived of God himself as guiding our prayers—even in their inchoate form—the same way parents coach their infants' first attempts at speech and are able to grasp the meaning of their earliest words, although strangers might discern nothing coming from the children but meaningless babble.

God gives himself to us unconditionally and is always inviting us into deeper communion with him. Unconditional love is an end in itself, and so is prayer. *Praying is not a means to something else*, not mainly a way of acquiring positive emotions, peace of mind, stronger faith, or even the miraculous healing of a friend we're praying for. Such things, as well as other experiences and gifts from God, may well come as what we call "answers" to prayer, but in a sense these answers are only by-products of prayer, not its ultimate purpose. *The ultimate purpose of prayer is to draw us into increasingly closer union with God.*

It might seem paradoxical to say, as I do, that petition is the *foundation* of prayer, but that receiving what we ask for is not the ultimate *purpose* of prayer. Here's an analogy drawn from the world of sports that might be helpful. Like all analogies it's inexact, but I hope it will illustrate the point I want to make. A professional football player's *ultimate purpose* is to play his position well and help his team win. If the football player wants to achieve the goal of helping his team win, he needs to listen to his coach, study the playbook, practice hard, take care of his health, and do a lot of strength training. He needs to understand his position perfectly, be a good team player, and stay physically strong, quick, and agile. The foundational qualities he needs to develop—understanding of his position, good relationships with teammates, and physical fitness—are essential. But the goal, the ultimate purpose of his study and training is to help his team win games. In a similar way, a life of prayer—whose foundation is faithful petition for our own needs and intercession for the needs of others (which will sometimes be fully realized and sometimes not)—is an essential *prerequisite* for all who make their life's journey with Jesus. The destination of that journey, however, the ultimate *purpose* of prayer, is ever-increasing intimacy with God.

If there are any Bible verses we are able to quote, or at least paraphrase, from memory, chances are good that many of them come from the collection of Jesus' sayings called the Sermon on the Mount (Matthew 5–7). The most familiar part of the sermon is the first ten verses, usually known as the

"Beatitudes." I want to draw attention to one of these Beatitudes: "Blessed are the pure in heart, for they will see God" (Matt 5:8). Translating one Greek word somewhat more exactly, we might say, "*Happy* are the pure in heart, for they will see God!" I think purity of heart is *spiritual integrity*. We have purity of heart when what is "on our inside" is also manifested "on our outside." Integrity is essential for people who want to follow Jesus and imitate his life. There needs to be a one-to-one correspondence between our convictions and our attitudes, our beliefs, and our way of life. The opposite of integrity is *hypocrisy*, which is pretending, playacting, "putting on."

It's important, then, for our prayers to have integrity. When we pray, we must explicitly open our minds, hearts, self-perceptions, emotions, desires, frustrations, and fears to God—everything about ourselves, holding nothing back. Of course, we believe that God knows all this without our actually *saying* anything. As I already pointed out, God is the one to whom "all hearts are open, all desires known, and from whom no secrets are hid."[22] But *to turn our deepest thoughts and feelings into words articulated in prayer* is a way of intentionally acknowledging and choosing to live with that reality. That's why petition is the foundation of our prayer, because our sincere requests to God disclose our true selves. I also think honesty in prayer must include openness with God about our frustrations and disappointments, including our disappointments *with him*—and there are times when all of us who pray have felt disappointment with God.

To use myself as an example, there have been times when I have prayed for weeks for another person's needs, such as healing or guidance or reconciliation after a broken relationship. When I have not discerned a response from God to my persistent prayers, I have felt compelled to pour out my frustration to him. Because I have kept a prayer journal for more than thirty years, these prayers of frustration have usually been written down in my journal, made concrete by pen and ink on paper.

Praying this way was prompted by reflection on the Psalms, which are really a collection of poetic prayers by devout children of Israel—including King David—compiled over five centuries. I look at how those ancient people of deep faith in God who wrote the psalms dealt not only with their joy in the Lord, but with their sorrow, frustration, and even anger at God—remaining always reverent, but practicing integrity. Purity of heart requires getting in touch with our honest feelings, even when our feelings are not pleasant or pious. There are ways to do this, as the psalms demonstrate, in which the author effectively says, "Lord, why don't you do something to

---

22. From the Collect for Purity, near the beginning of the Eucharist in most Anglican rites.

save us? Why do you remain silent? We're dying here! Why do you leave us in this wretched situation? You have power to deliver us, and you have delivered us in the past. Why do you now abandon us to our enemies? Arise, O Lord, and help us!"[23] Following the example of such psalms, I have written words like these in my prayer journal:

> Father, I know your love is unconditional and your compassion for N. is far greater than mine. Why do my prayers for him seem to be going without an answer? Or is your answer simply *no*? I'm trying to encourage N. to trust you, yet all he is experiencing seems to be more pain, frustration, and spiritual darkness. I want to serve you, Father, but I cannot understand what's going on. Help me, please. Do something I can see. Say something I can hear. Illuminate my heart. Deliver me from this frustration!

People *do* get angry at God, though few of us want to admit it. Such anger is not sin. It's human; it's normal. All children get angry at their parents sometimes. Their anger may be misplaced or simply juvenile, but they feel it, and it affects their relationship with their mothers and fathers. Good parents know when their children are angry and frustrated, and they know how to deal with angry children. They do not react with hostility and say, "How dare you feel that way and say such things to us?" Instead, they listen, they explain—at the level of the child's understanding—and they stay close, no matter how the child may act out. In my experience, openness to God about not only my love for him and the desires of my heart, but also my anger, frustration, and disappointment has been rewarded by growth in faith and an increasing assurance that God is committed to me, always deeply engaged with me, no matter what my emotional or mental state might be. We can honestly say: God believes in us.

"Pray constantly," Saint Paul says (1Thess 5:17). This is possible only for those who understand that *prayer is any deliberate activity meant to turn us toward God.* We may turn ourselves toward God if we're driving in traffic, look off and see a nearby mountain range capped with snow, and say to ourselves and to God, "This is my Father's world." We turn ourselves towards God if we're flipping through the pages of a magazine in the dentist's office, notice an advertisement that pictures a mother or a father cuddling an infant, and think, "God, that's how you hold me!"

We turn ourselves towards God when we take a lesson from Brother Lawrence. Lawrence was an ex-soldier and humble lay brother who worked

---

23. See, e.g., portions of Psalms 9, 10, 44, 74, and 102.

as a dishwasher and, later, as a shoemaker in his monastery. For him, times of work, times of rest, and times of worship seemed all the same, all of them occasions for communion with God, because he chose to think of all his tasks as jobs he was doing personally for God. Lawrence told people that as far as he was concerned, prayer consisted totally and simply of understanding God as always present with him.[24]

We don't usually think of our acts of mercy as being a form of *prayer*, but I believe we are turning ourselves toward God when we commit our time to hands-on, compassionate love for others—whether it's helping at a homeless shelter, working in a food bank, teaching physically handicapped people to ski, or even simply taking time to befriend a lonely person and give that solitary soul our undivided attention. We turn ourselves toward God when we recognize the truth of the incarnation and see Jesus in the faces of our neighbors, our sisters and brothers in need. When we do that, we understand that God shares our human condition, and that Jesus is now and ever has been our neighbor.[25] Jesus makes this clear in his parable of the Great Judgment:

> When the Son of Man comes in his glory, and all the angels with him, then he will sit on the throne of his glory. All the nations will be gathered before him, and he will separate people one from another as a shepherd separates the sheep from the goats, and he will put the sheep at his right hand and the goats at the left. Then the king will say to those at his right hand, "Come, you that are blessed by my Father, inherit the kingdom prepared for you from the foundation of the world; for I was hungry and you gave me food, I was thirsty and you gave me something to drink, I was a stranger and you welcomed me, I was naked and you gave me clothing, I was sick and you took care of me, I was in prison and you visited me." Then the righteous will answer him, "Lord, when was it that we saw you hungry and gave you food, or thirsty and gave you something to drink? And when was it that we saw you a stranger and welcomed you, or naked and gave you clothing? And when was it that we saw you sick or in prison and visited you?" And the king will answer them, "Truly I tell you, just as you did it to one of the least of these who are members of my family, you did it to me" (Matt 25:31–40 NRSV).

Louis Évely writes, "It is the great Christian truth that you are no nearer to God than you are to your neighbor."[26]

---

24. Brother Lawrence, *Practice*, 24.
25. Ibid., 71–75.
26. Évely, *We Are*, 72.

Finding the Way

༄ ༄ ༄

For Your Reflection

After reading chapter 5, "Responding to God's Love: Prayer"

- Read this passage from the Gospel according to Luke slowly and thoughtfully, perhaps doing so aloud the first time and then silently. Read it several times if you wish.

    > I say to you, Ask, and it will be given to you; search, and you will find; knock, and the door will be opened for you. *For everyone who asks receives, and everyone who searches finds, and for everyone who knocks, the door will be opened.* Is there anyone among you who, if your child asks for a fish, will give a snake instead of a fish? Or if the child asks for an egg, will give a scorpion? If you then, who are evil, know how to give good gifts to your children, how much more will the heavenly Father give the Holy Spirit to those who ask him! (Luke 11:9–13 NRSV, italics added)

    After reading the whole passage reflectively, spend time meditating on the italicized verse. Ask God how to apply it to your own life. Make this the focus of your prayer for one day. You can do the same meditation more than once, choosing a different sentence for meditation each time.

- At the time when you usually pray, instead of following your customary pattern, take out a sheet of paper and write at the top, "Dear God, I thank you for, . . . " and then list everything that comes immediately to mind for which you're thankful. Include little things as well as big things. Being thankful for a magnificent sunset is just as important as being thankful for your home and family. Being thankful for memories is good, too. Don't stop writing until you're forced to stop in order to think whether there is something else to add. When that happens, you're at the end of this prayer exercise.

- On a day when you're very busy and it looks as if there is no time to pray, or perhaps on a day when you don't feel like praying or think you can't pray, reflect on the phrases from the Our Father printed below. You can do this driving the car or walking down the street or standing in the checkout line at a supermarket. Anytime. Start at the beginning

Responding to God's Love: Prayer

or start in the middle, think about the whole prayer or just part of it. After each phrase, think about what that means to you. If you want to use the contemporary English version of the prayer, that's fine.

- Our Father who art in heaven
- Hallowed be thy name
- Thy kingdom come
- Thy will be done on earth as it is in heaven
- Give us this day our daily bread
- Forgive us our trespasses
- As we forgive those who trespass against us
- And lead us not into temptation
- But deliver us from evil
- For thine is the kingdom, and the power, and the glory forever

- Go for a walk around your neighborhood or in the woods or by a stream or on a mountain trail. As you start your walk, pray, "Lord, show me something. Speak to me through what I see or touch or smell." Then, as you walk, don't let your mind wander, but rather stay open and use your physical senses to experience the world around you—notice things small and close at hand, as well as things further off. Look at growing things, trees and flowers, birds and animals, other people, clouds, a lake or river, hills and mountains, farmland . . . *everything*. Feel the wind. Smell the air. Trust that God will draw your attention to something significant, and when that happens, pause and let God "speak" to you. This may happen more than once on your walk. Remember, this is not a hike to get exercise but a prayer walk, so don't try to work up a sweat.

- Deliberately open your heart to God. Even though we know that nothing about us is hidden from God, it's important for us to open ourselves intentionally to the Father. After you have settled yourself in the place where you usually pray, in complete privacy, say something like this: "Father, I want to open my whole heart to you, my thoughts, my feelings, my hopes and wants, my fears and my hurts. I want to confess my sins. I don't want to hide anything from you." Then tell the Lord what's on your mind and in your heart. Unburden yourself, and do so without fear. This is a prayer that might best be spoken aloud, though only when there is no possibility that someone else might hear your voice.

Chapter 6

Responding to God's Love: Loving Your Neighbor as Yourself

And behold, a lawyer stood up to put him to the test, saying, "Teacher, what shall I do to inherit eternal life?" He said to him, "What is written in the law? How do you read?" And he answered, "You shall love the Lord your God with all your heart, and with all your soul, and with all your strength, and with all your mind; and your neighbor as yourself." And he said to him, "You have answered right; do this, and you will live." But he, desiring to justify himself, said to Jesus, "And who is my neighbor?"

—LUKE 10:25–29

IF WE'VE DETERMINED TO follow Jesus on the journey of life and live as his disciples, we already know that a disciple's goal is to reproduce the life of the Master.[1] One of the obvious aspects of Jesus' behavior was the empathy and compassion that caused him to be called "the Man for Others."[2] His life embodied wholehearted devotion to God, and that love for God was closely paralleled by love for everyone around him. We may not have recognized it when we began our journey with Jesus, but we can't be on the trail with him for long before we learn that this journey is not going to be mainly about our personal healing, spiritual growth, and self-improvement. All of that may well happen, but walking this path with Christ isn't a kind of thera-

---

1. To "reproduce the life of the Master" means to replicate Jesus' pattern of life, not its historic details. This is "the imitation of Christ."

2. Dietrich Bonhoeffer, the German pastor who was imprisoned and ultimately executed by the Nazis, expressed in his surviving letters the desire to write a book about Jesus that would be called *The Man for Others*. See Beck, "Letters," n.p.

peutic process. Its purpose is not mainly to reorganize our lives so we have greater peace of mind, more spiritual energy, and happy, positive feelings about ourselves. Our *Abba* loves us, but God's grace is given for purposes that reach far beyond us.

To know we're the beloved children of God is a wonderful and essential thing, but the purpose of God's love working in us is to shape us gradually, step by step, into the likeness of his Son, Jesus—the "Man for Others." This is a process; it doesn't happen quickly. But if we trust God and accept his love, we're positioned to grow into our destiny as his children. Our *Abba*'s love, poured into our hearts by his Spirit, is the resource that empowers us to be like Jesus, to choose to love as he loves.

Pastors sometimes hear people ask, "Why didn't God just program us to love others? God is omnipotent, isn't he? Why didn't God just make us so we'd be instinctively altruistic and compassionate?" This is similar to the question, "Why does God permit evil?" The simple answer is that God wants us to be his children, not his machines. We who are parents love our children as unconditionally as we possibly can—but we always have hopes and dreams for their lives. If we love them unconditionally, though, we refrain from trying to stage-manage their futures to make them fit our agenda. We want our children to be free to set their own courses through life—supporting them as much as we can, but not dictating what directions they take.

By the same token, God our Father does not compel us to live the life he wants for us. If God had wanted robots rather than children, then we would be robots. We live in a contingent universe full of occasions that force us to make choices, some of which will be good and some bad. Our *Abba* delights in our freedom and never forces us to do the right thing, even though he knows we're making bad decisions. God loves us, invites us, warns us, and disciplines us, but never forces us. We are free moral agents, and we live with the consequences of our choices, good or bad. No one can read the Old Testament story of God's covenant love for Israel and Israel's frequent episodes of failure and faithlessness without perceiving that God does not compel his children to do his will. God wants us to do his will, but only out of our free choice. The prayer "Thy will be done" is the best of all prayers, but that prayer only counts if we mean it. God isn't an indulgent grandpa who will shower us with favor just because we tell him things he wants to hear, whether we mean them or not.

Responding to God's Love: Loving Your Neighbor as Yourself

To put it simply, the life God wants for us is the kind of life Christ lived on earth and lives in eternity, the life of the kingdom of God. And that kingdom life is lived in community, as part of a vast family, the family of God. That means our journey with Jesus is not only about developing or improving our private relationship with God, but also about linking our lives in love with all the rest of God's family.

If asked, "Would you like to have eternal life," few people are likely to say, "No, I'm not interested." If eternal life is an option, pretty close to 100 percent of us would like to have it. That makes the question the lawyer asks in the quotation from Luke printed at the heading of this chapter as relevant now as when he asked it. The so-called lawyer in this story is not the sort of lawyer with whom we're familiar. This lawyer is a Jewish religious scholar, a scribe, an expert in the law of Moses. And his question doesn't mean "What must I do to live forever?" Eternal life refers to the kind of life God wants his children to enjoy, both now and in the age to come, life in the kingdom of God. It's about the quality of that life as much as it is about its duration.[3]

Being talented at this kind of debate, Jesus tosses a question right back to the lawyer, "What do you read in the law?" The man then gives an answer that other gospels credit to Jesus himself, and which is sometimes called "the Lord's Summary" of the law: "You shall love the Lord your God with all your heart, and with all your soul, and with all your strength, and with all your mind; and your neighbor as yourself" (Luke 10:27).

Jesus says, "That's the right answer. Do that, and you will live." Notice, he doesn't say "Do that, and you'll go to heaven when you die." He says, "Do that, and you will live"—that is, you'll have a life that's really Life—with a capital "L"—right now, not just in the hereafter.

For the lawyer, there remains one small detail he wants Jesus to explain. If he is required by the law of God to love his neighbor as himself, he'd like to know the extent of his legal obligation. Therefore, he asks, "Exactly who is my neighbor?" Why does he ask Jesus this? Is it merely an academic question, arising out of concern about the specific words used in the Torah, or does it come from more personal, private considerations? The

---

3. Wright, *How God*, 41–45. Wright points out that the expression *zoē aiōnios*, usually translated into English as "everlasting life" or "eternal life," really means "life of the age to come" or "life of God's new age." Wright says that it is not "a promise of a timeless heavenly bliss," but rather of life in a new age of justice, peace, and healing.

scribe wants to hear what Jesus thinks are the limits of the legal category identified as that of "neighbor." Perhaps Jesus thinks neighbors are literally people who live in one's own village. Or perhaps neighbors are all of one's fellow Jews, or one's fellow Jews plus any Gentiles living within the Jewish community. The scribe knows that if Jesus says the category of *neighbor* has no limits, then Jesus is saying that the law of God—at least in his eyes—requires the questioner to love everyone else just as much as he loves himself. But who could possibly do that?

To answer the man's question, Jesus tells the parable that people all over the world now know as the story of the Good Samaritan (Luke 10:21–37). "Good Samaritan" has entered the popular vocabulary, among non-Christians as well as Christians, as the name for a person who goes out of the way to help a stranger. Jesus puts a twist in his story by making its hero the representative of a category of people despised by the Jews, and who despised the Jews in return. That must have shocked his Jewish audience. It would have been like a white preacher in the Deep South in 1860 (or even 1960) choosing to use the description of a black slave's compassion as an example of Christian character—and then, to make things worse, choosing to compare the slave's kindness with the heartlessness of some white clergymen. Folks in the pews would have been outraged by such a sermon, and the preacher would have been on his way out of town before the following Sunday.

At the end of the parable, Jesus asks the scribe, "Which of the three—the priest, the Levite, or the Samaritan—do you think showed himself a neighbor to the man who fell among robbers?" And the scribe replies, "The one who showed him mercy." To show mercy means to provide whatever help is needed. If I show mercy to another person, I identify myself as that person's neighbor. The person need not live on my block or belong to my family, ethnic group, club, or church. By this reply, Jesus tells the lawyer that he understands the law as requiring the children of God to love everyone as much as they love themselves.

Richard B. Hays explains the significance of the parable of the Good Samaritan this way:

> The point is that we are called upon to *become* neighbors to those who are helpless, going beyond conventional conceptions of duty to provide life-sustaining aid to those whom we might not have regarded as worthy of our compassion. . . . Jesus calls upon us to widen [the scope of our moral concern] by showing mercy and

Responding to God's Love: Loving Your Neighbor as Yourself

actively intervening on behalf of the helpless. The Samaritan is a paradigm of love that goes beyond ordinary obligation and thus *creates* a neighbor relation where none existed before. The concluding word of the parable addresses us all: "Go, and do likewise."[4]

Jesus' lesson for his questioner was clear, and it should be clear to us: If we really want to live, if we want to "get a life," as people say, then we should imitate the Good Samaritan. "Go and do likewise." Be compassionate people. Be good neighbors. Compassion isn't just a feeling; it's a decision to act on that feeling, putting our personal resources on the line and thinking about what we might be able to do once we get involved. If we want to experience the sense of fulfillment that comes from knowing we're living in the center of God's will, we choose to meet the needs of the needy, even if the needy are very different from us, even if we never laid eyes on them before, even if helping them interrupts our routine, and even if it costs us money. This is the message of Jesus: Choose to imitate the Good Samaritan; choose to be people who so identify with the needs and hurts of those around us that the care we give them is exactly the care we'd want to receive if we were in their shoes. This means living the golden rule: "Do to others as you would have them do to you" (Luke 6:31 NRSV).

We can only love because God first loved us. The love we give back to God is always a response to God's love for us, and loving our neighbor is a way of loving God, a response to divine love that is as definitive as worship or prayer. Indeed, the commandment to love our neighbor tests whether we actually love God at all. That's why the first and second great commandments are inseparable. I am touched by what Louis Évely says: "We are only as near to God as we are to our neighbor. You are no nearer to God than you are to your neighbor, because God is your neighbor, within the reach of your hand. Within the reach of your love."[5] That's true, but it's only one side of the coin. Évely adds,

> If I am no nearer to God than I am to my neighbor, then I am as near to God as I am to my neighbor. Consequently, all that I would do for God, I can do for him. . . . I wish to smile at God, then let me smile at my neighbor. I can give God something to eat and drink. I can comfort God. I can pay a visit to God. I can write Him a letter. I can set a nice table. I can cook a nice meal. And for God! What joy! . . . And, on the Last Day, He will say to me, "You smiled at

4. Hayes, *Moral*, 451 (italics in original).
5. Évely, *We Are*, 72–73.

Finding the Way

me, you visited me, you took care of me. You set the table for me with love, you did the washing for me with love. You cooked good meals for me with love. . . . You have lived with me with love."[6]

Typical Christians have heard the parable of the Good Samaritan so often we automatically perceive it as a simple story with an obvious moral lesson, because we habitually identify ourselves with the Samaritan. We imagine we'd do just what he did if we were confronted on a lonely and dangerous stretch of road with a poor victim of highway robbery. Thinking like that allows us to stay in our comfort zone. We're "good people." But there's plenty of evidence that we might well be deluding ourselves, since our society is clearly full of otherwise decent citizens who do not imitate the Good Samaritan, even when they have a clear opportunity. Anyone who monitors the 24/7 news cycle for a while will encounter story after story about bystanders who remained inert while others were robbed right in front of them, or assaulted, or even shot dead. They were surprised, shocked, paralyzed with fear, unsure of what to do, or "just didn't want to get involved."

We might grasp the meaning of Jesus' famous parable better if we make an effort to identify ourselves with the victim rather than with the Good Samaritan. Imagine that Jesus is telling a story about us lying by the highway, stripped, robbed, nearly dead, and desperately needing somebody—anybody, friend or foe—to have compassion on us before we bleed to death. Or, if that seems too far-fetched, then just imagine we're stranded in a broken-down old Volkswagen on a busy interstate, with no way to call for help. Has that ever happened to you? It happened to me forty years ago on I-95 just outside New York City. It was rush hour on a holiday weekend, and I was very scared as I sat in my broken car praying for help. Surely, some of the hundreds of people who speeded past me on that Memorial Day weekend in 1972 were serious Christians. But none of them even slowed down. Finally, a New Jersey state trooper came along and told me he'd radio for a tow truck to come out from Hoboken. He also advised me to get out and go stand a distance away from my little car, because it was likely to be hit by another vehicle in the heavy traffic. I took his suggestion.

Loving other people the way we love ourselves requires that we identify with them, whoever they are, and perceive that we and they are

---

6. Ibid., 76–77.

Responding to God's Love: Loving Your Neighbor as Yourself

alike—children of God to whom life can deal out unexpected wounds and bruises. We are committed to making our life journey guided by Jesus, walking in his footsteps as disciples and seeking to imitate his example. We read in the gospels that from the very beginning of his ministry, Jesus identifies personally with needy people. We see a picture of him going down to the Jordan River where his cousin John is telling people to turn from sins, come to him for baptism, and start living a new life. John's message is persuasive. Throngs of men and women, old and young, soldiers, tax collectors, even priests and Levites and Pharisees, are coming down to the water to be cleansed of sin and make a fresh start.

I'm speculating, but I think Jesus might have said to himself, as he stood watching the crowds wading into the river day after day, "These are my people. My life's work is to serve them, help them, save them." Jesus was a righteous man by anybody's standards. Not a criminal. Not a hypocrite. Not a fraud. But he chose to identify with people who were those things and worse. Jesus could have moved to Jerusalem, taken up residence near the temple, and become a rabbi or a scribe—identifying with the most pious and respected men of his generation. He could have had a distinguished career, according to the highest standards of that pious society. But instead, he chose to identify himself with the outcast, the morally marginalized, and the failures, rather than with the esteemed and learned sages. He had empathy for people who had experienced rejection. He sensed how they felt; he knew what they needed. So, he put himself in their shoes and determined to do whatever it took to give them hope. The gospels portray Jesus joining the sinners and plunging with them into the waters of the Jordan, fulfilling what he discerns to be the purpose of his life. When he does that, the heavens open, the Holy Spirit descends upon him like a dove, and the voice of the Father says, "You are my Son, the Beloved, with you I am well pleased."[7]

The central figure of our faith is the Son of God, who came to give us eternal life. Jesus identified with all our needs as human beings—not only our physical needs, but our loneliness, our desire for a shepherd to guide us, our hunger for truth, our desire to be loved just as we are, our fear of death, and our hope for forgiveness. If we who choose to walk life's road with Jesus are serious about wanting to live the eternal life he talked about, life in the kingdom of God, then we will imitate him by opening our hearts

---

7. Luke 3:22 NRSV. The baptism of Jesus is described in the Synoptics and alluded to in John. See Matt 3:1–17; Mark 1:1–11; Luke 3:1–22; and John 1:11–34.

Finding the Way

to the pain, grief, hunger, and fear of those who share our world—reaching out in mercy to love them as we love ourselves.

Because we live in the Age of Therapy, when we hear the expression "love your neighbor as yourself," we automatically tend to psychologize the phrase, and begin wondering what constitutes healthy self-love. This sends us down the wrong road. To love my neighbor as myself does not require me to arrive at a mental health–oriented definition of self-love. In the biblical context, to love oneself simply means to take care of one's needs—of whatever sort they may be—in a natural way. To love myself means, then, to provide for myself food and drink when I'm hungry and thirsty, a bath when I feel dirty, a coat when I'm cold, a house to live in, transportation to work, money as needed, and medical care when I'm sick.

Whatever we regard as *necessities* for ourselves, we should wish to provide for others who lack them. For example, if I've been injured in an accident, it's necessary for me to have medical treatment. If I am to hold a job and support my dependents, it's necessary for me to have an education. If I work outside my home, it's necessary for me to have transportation to work. If I am not to be a soulless drudge, it's necessary for me to have opportunities for recreation and intellectual stimulus. Loving your neighbor as yourself can be very practical. If my neighbor has no way to get to his job every day and I'm able to give him a ride, buy him a bus pass or a bike, or maybe give him my old car to drive, what would Jesus suggest I do? If the young couple in the apartment next door have not had an evening out in a year because they can't afford a babysitter, much less a restaurant tab, what would Jesus want me to do? There should be no debate about the answers to those questions.

But there is another perspective on providing for our neighbor the sorts of things we need for ourselves, a perspective that takes into consideration needs beyond the merely material. The most pressing needs of our neighbors are likely to be physical ones, the sort caused by social conditions such as poverty or disease. However, if we permit our minds to be shaped by the gospel of Christ, if we see our neighbors through the eyes of Jesus, we soon come to recognize that neither our own needs nor the needs of our neighbors are *exclusively* physical.

Christian political philosopher Glenn Tinder writes that we fail to recognize the unique glory of human beings if we understand ourselves as called upon by Christ to love our neighbors only by providing them with material things of the sort required even by animals. Naturally, animal needs are basic, because we can't live unless they're met. But non-physical needs have a moral priority in the sense that we who are created in the image of God cannot be fully human unless our spiritual and social needs are also met. Love for neighbors, therefore, must include more than merely physical aid. It must involve *inviting them into community with us*. Tinder says this about the love Christ calls us to demonstrate to others:

> When urgent physical needs have been met, love consists in speaking the truth, as one understands it, and in listening to those who are speaking the truth as they understand it. *When love performs these acts, it calls forth community.* We [ask], What is community? Can we not say that community is what comes into existence when people speak to one another, and listen, in an effort to discern the truth? . . . Community does not consist solely in the possession of truth but also in the search for truth.[8]

The need for community, the shared quest for truth that demands openness and dialogue with one another, is a need that disciples who want to love their neighbors as themselves will recognize, because we perceive the same need within ourselves. We need hospitality.[9] We need friendship. We need someone to treat us with dignity and listen to what we say. We need other people to be our partners in the great endeavors to which we feel called. This need for community is partly what impelled us to join the long procession of seekers walking on the upward way with Jesus, listening to him together and learning the truth about God and ourselves.

American culture admires rugged individualism and demonstrates great respect for the so-called self-made man or woman. But the gospel's emphasis on community is unmistakable. Jesus is shown as busy creating a community, drawing disciples into relationship with him and with one another. Our journey with Jesus must be made—if it is to be made at all—in company with others. In the gospels, Jesus relates to his twelve closest disciples as a community of people whose lives are spiritually interconnected. He does not treat them the way a university professor today would treat twelve members of an advanced seminar group, as students with a common career goal, but no other necessary bond among them. We follow the One

---

8. Tinder, *Political*, 121 (italics added).

9. "If there is any concept worth restoring to its original depth and evocative potential, it is the concept of hospitality. It is one of the richest biblical terms that can deepen and broaden our insight into our relationships to our fellow human beings. Old and New Testament stories not only show how serious our obligation is to welcome the stranger in our home, but they also tell us that guests are carrying precious gifts with them, which they are eager to reveal to a receptive host." Nouwen, *Reaching Out*, 41–42.

who says, "I am the way, and the truth, and the life. No one comes to the Father except through me" (John 14:6).

Recognition of the truth we experience in Jesus needs to be coupled with willingness to apply that truth in our behavior. The gospel is not proclaimed in order to provide subject matter for leisurely discussion, but to give practical guidance for daily living. The contemporary version of the Bible called *The Message* puts a familiar warning from the Letter of James this way: "Don't fool yourself into thinking that you are a listener when you are anything but, letting the Word go in one ear and out the other. Act on what you hear! Those who hear and don't act are like those who glance in the mirror, walk away, and two minutes later have no idea who they are, what they look like" (Jas 1:21–24).

As we think about what it means to love our neighbors as ourselves, it's important to recognize that the New Testament does not teach us to love our fellow Christians with greater generosity than we do others. Loving our neighbors is not distinguished from loving our fellow Christians. The point of the parable of the Good Samaritan is that there is no limit to our obligation to love others. We don't owe a higher level of compassion to other Christians than to anyone else. All human beings are our sisters and brothers and neighbors.[10] When we hear Jesus speaking about love, he speaks not of different loves, but of one—the same love for the brother, the neighbor, and even the enemy—a love expressed in deeds of service.

At the Last Supper, when he humbles himself to wash their feet—the one lowly task a disciple would have refused to perform even for his teacher—Jesus gives the Twelve a word of instruction, which he calls a new commandment. He says, "Just as I have loved you, so you also should love one another. By this everyone will know that you are my disciples, if you have love for one another" (John 13:34–35 NRSV). Jesus did not mean for this mutual love to be restricted to other disciples, but rather that the practice of indiscriminate, compassionate charity towards all should thereafter be known as *the* defining characteristic of his followers.[11] History attests that this is precisely what happened.

---

10. When he addressed himself to the Athenian assembly on the Areopagus, Paul said, "[God] is not far from each one of us. For 'In him we live and move and have our being;' as even some of your own poets have said, 'For we too are his offspring'" (Acts 17:27b–28). The Greek word *genos*, translated "offspring," is the word for "family."

11. It is legitimate, simply in terms of language, to speak of love of neighbors (or of enemies) as charity, because such love is not an emotional state, but rather a chosen form of behavior: benevolence without expectation of reciprocation, doing good for another

Responding to God's Love: Loving Your Neighbor as Yourself

The neighbors of early Christians were struck by how the Christians not only loved the other members of their fellowship, but their pagan neighbors as well, reaching out in mercy even to strangers in need. Athenagoras of Athens, writing around AD 176, said, "With us [i.e., among Christians] you will find unlettered people, tradesmen and old women, who, though unable to express in words the advantages of our teaching, demonstrate by acts the value of their principles. For they do not rehearse speeches; but evidence good deeds. *When struck, they do not strike back; when robbed, they do not sue; to those who ask, they give; and they love their neighbors as themselves.*"[12]

Two hundred years later, after the conversion of Constantine and the recognition of Christianity by the Roman state, Constantine's nephew the emperor Julian—called "the Apostate"—abandoned Christianity and attempted to restore worship of the pagan gods. Julian tried to shame pagans into imitating the compassion of Christians, whom he habitually called "atheists." This is shown by a letter he wrote in AD 362 to the pagan high priest of Galatia: "Why do we not observe how the kindness of the atheists [i.e., Christians] to strangers, their care for the burial of their dead, and the sobriety of their lifestyle has done the most to increase atheism [i.e., Christianity]? . . . It is disgraceful when no Jew is a beggar and the impious Galileans [i.e., Christians] support our poor in addition to their own; everyone is able to see that our coreligionists are in want of aid from us. . . . *Do not therefore let others outdo us in good deeds while we ourselves are disgraced by laziness.*"[13]

Concern for social justice—the well-being of all people, the good of others and not just our own family or economic or social class—is an aspect of loving our neighbors. This has been borne out by the church's practice since earliest times. As we reflect on our responsibilities as followers of Jesus, the gospel clearly teaches that we live among neighbors to whom we owe a debt of love, or of charity, if we prefer that word. If we look at our life obligations in a strictly economic sense, the message of the parable of the Good Samaritan can be seen as leaving us with potentially vast responsibilities, because the world is full of needy neighbors. If we have neighbors who need our help, spending surplus assets on a new car or an expensive vacation or a second home could seem morally problematic. This is the attitude Francis of Assisi adopted when he gave up his inheritance to become

---

with no reward anticipated for oneself. The Latin *caritas*, which gives us the English word charity, is one of the common ways the Vulgate translates the Greek word *agapē*.

12. Athenagoras, *Supplicatio*, 11.1–3, in Meeks, *Origins*, 121 (italics added).
13. Julian, *Works*, 61–70 (italics added).

Finding the Way

a servant of the poor.[14] If I take the gospel seriously, I must confess that my needy neighbor has a right to turn to me for aid, and nothing in the words of Jesus implies that I should pass judgment on his worthiness before I decide to help. If I am defrauded, I entrust myself—and my neighbor—to the providence of God.

Serious Christians are called to weigh these moral claims as we make decisions about the use of our personal resources. I raise this issue only as a reminder that to persevere in following Jesus with sincerity and conviction means ultimately to commit ourselves to imitating a man whose destiny was to lay down his life for his friends, and who says to those friends, "If any want to become my followers, let them deny themselves and take up their cross and follow me. For those who want to save their life will lose it, and those who lose their life for my sake, and for the sake of the gospel, will save it" (Mark 8:34b–35 NRSV).

The circumstances of modern society raise issues that cannot be easily disposed of. For example, is the commandment to love our neighbors as ourselves somehow attenuated, or perhaps even eliminated, in our time because the civil government taxes us and uses that money to provide assistance to those in need? Because the government provides food stamps, income assistance, and basic medical care or other social welfare benefits to the poor, does that relieve followers of Jesus of the duty to address the needs of our neighbors? Instead of direct, compassionate aid, do we simply hand our needy neighbors a booklet listing the addresses and phone numbers of local social agencies? Many people fall through the cracks or are unqualified under the law for public assistance, but nevertheless have legitimate needs. What about them? There are severe needs for which there is no form of public assistance available. Furthermore, as I indicated earlier, love for our neighbors entails more than practical assistance. It asks that we link our lives with theirs, that we draw them into community with us.

Following Christ, imitating Christ, becomes intensely challenging when we consider Jesus' mandate to love our neighbors as ourselves and to do for others as we would wish them to do for us. Jesus makes self-denial and willingness to take up our cross the condition of discipleship. Notice that Jesus proposes no doctrinal test for his disciples, only a lifestyle test. We have a choice. We don't have to follow Jesus; we don't have to take

---

14. See *Encyclopaedia Britannica*, "Saint Francis of Assisi," n.p.

up the cross. But if we will not take up our cross, then we can't actually be Jesus' followers. We'll have to settle for being his admirers rather than his disciples and find ourselves watching him from a distance, crying out, "Lord, I can go with you only so far. I am not able to pay the price it takes to become your disciple. It's too high." The truth is that we can be church members without being disciples. Authentic disciples will imitate the life of the One who says that he came "not to be served, but to serve, and to give his life a ransom for many" (Matt 20:28). Authentic disciples will choose to take up the cross.

The decisive question for us is this: Can Christians who are holding jobs and raising families in twenty-first-century American society be authentic disciples? Can we take up the cross and follow Jesus? If we have only our personal strength, will power, and moral fiber to enable us, the answer is no. But I believe the answer is yes, we can, if we cooperate with the grace of God and let Jesus reshape our value system. We don't have to give away everything we own and we don't have to renounce our families and become monks or hermits. But we do have to put all our resources at the Lord's disposal and no longer live in bondage to money or things or power or status.

If we think deeply about the cross that Jesus carried from Pilate's tribunal out to the hill called Golgotha, we recognize that it was a cross that did not really belong to him. The cross was the Roman instrument of punishment for a slave who had made an attempt on the life of his master or for a rebel against the authority of Rome. Jesus was neither. He was the innocent Lamb of God offering himself to bear the sins of the world, the Son of God who so identified with our sinful human state that he took our humanity upon himself in order to set us free and make us his sisters and brothers. Jesus did not deserve the cross or punishment of any kind. The cross he chose to bear was, both literally and theologically, for others. For us.

On that understanding, then, what is *my* cross? It can't be my arthritis or my job or the people who don't seem to understand me. My cross can only be the burden I choose to bear, the price I choose to pay, for the sake of others, my neighbors. My cross is the means by which I die to my egocentric self and begin to live in the kingdom of God.

Finding the Way

↭ ↭ ↭

For Your Reflection

*After reading chapter 6,
"Responding to God's Love: Loving Your Neighbor as Yourself"*

- When you read, "You shall love the Lord your God with all your heart, and with all your soul, and with all your strength, and with all your mind; and your neighbor as yourself," which part feels easier, loving God or loving your neighbor? Why do you think that is?
- Remember a time when you were in need of a Good Samaritan and one appeared. What effect did that have on you?
- Name five times you have been a Good Samaritan for someone. How did that make you feel?
- Remember the last time you thought about being a Good Samaritan, but decided not to act. What stopped you?
- What is the most personally costly thing you have ever done for someone who was not a member of your immediate family? (Keep in mind that "costly" need not mean merely financial expense; it can include the spending of time or social costs as well.) What motivated you to do that? Did you have to be asked, or did you take the initiative?
- When you think about the needs of other people, with what needs do you most easily identify? With what needs do you have the greatest difficulty identifying?
- What kind of help feels easiest for you to offer a stranger in need? What kind is hardest?
- Show mercy to someone this week who is not a friend or relative.
- Pray for eyes to see what is your cross and the grace to take it up and walk with Jesus.

Chapter 7

Living with a Purpose

I appeal to you therefore, brothers and sisters, by the mercies of God, to present your bodies as a living sacrifice, holy and acceptable to God, which is your spiritual worship. Do not be conformed to this world, but be transformed by the renewing of your minds, so that you may discern what is the will of God—what is good and acceptable and perfect. For by the grace given to me I say to everyone among you not to think of yourself more highly than you ought to think, but to think with sober judgment, each according to the measure of faith that God has assigned.

—ROMANS 12:1–3 NRSV

I GREW UP IN a pretty conservative Calvinist church. I may be the only twelve-year-old who ever wrote a seventh grade English term paper on predestination. I don't know what my teacher thought when she read it, but the subject worried me a lot. I agonized about it. Even as a child I wondered: Is our sense of having choices in life only an illusion? Is everything already decided in advance by God? Are we just puppets manipulated from heaven by a string-pulling deity who determines everything we do, as well as our eternal destiny? If so, then what's the purpose of life? Why imagine our anguished choices matter?

Those concerns stuck with me and eventually led me to Anglicanism, where I learned that freedom to choose is a precious gift God has given us. In the biblical creation story, where it says God made Adam and Eve in his own image, it's the freedom to choose that made them most like God. God tells them not to eat the fruit of the tree in the center of the Garden, but they have a choice. They may obey or disobey, eat or not eat. That's the classic parable of mortal existence. It poses the great question, *how shall we use our freedom?*

Our choices matter. We have freedom to shape the direction of our lives as best we can, to set goals for ourselves and decide what we want our lives to mean. Of course this freedom operates within constraints. The circumstances of our upbringing and various forces in our culture and environment shape the choices we're at liberty to make. Context inclines us to choose certain things rather than others. For example, in these first decades of the twenty-first century, people who have grown up in America are more likely to be active in a church than are people who have grown up in Great Britain. And religious Americans are more likely to be Christians or Jews, while religious Indonesians are more likely to be Muslims. Culture and social context have an effect on human choices. In some cases, there may even be coercion, but we're still making choices. After all, courage to resist coercion is a decision, not just an emotional impulse.

If human beings were like machines, we would do neither good nor evil, right nor wrong. Freedom to choose is what makes us human and makes our behavior moral or immoral (or somewhere in between). God is not pulling strings, not making us do this or that. We are not robots. I believe that, in the biblical sense, *we were created to make choices.*

Shallow-minded skeptics think they've scored points on us when they say, "How can you believe in a good God when you see all the evil in this world?"[1] Nothing we do could be called good unless there were an equal option for choosing the opposite, what might—in contrast to good—be called *evil*. Choice between moral opposites, or from among the diversity of options that lie between the polar opposites, is essential if there are to be moral definitions at all. Choosing to feed the hungry or provide shelter for the homeless, or even give the thirsty little kid from next door a drink of water if he knocks on our door on a hot afternoon cannot be described as "good" in any sense, unless we also have freedom to ignore the needs of others and let them shift for themselves. And we can imagine an inverted moral universe where feeding the hungry might be identified as "evil" and letting them starve identified as "good." To say anything is good demands an awareness of its opposite.

---

1. Allen, *Theology*, 51–84. Part Two, "Suffering," offers helpful insights into the role of suffering and choice in human existence.

Living with a Purpose

There's a story in the Bible about a leper who falls on his knees in the road before Jesus, saying "*If you choose*, you can make me clean." Moved with pity, Jesus stretches out his hand, touches the leper, and says, "*I do choose*. Be made clean!" (Mark 1:41 NRSV, italics added). The law of Moses said contact with a leper would result in ritual defilement, but Jesus decides to reach out to the man anyway. Almost every day, we're faced with moral decisions: to do something good, something evil, or something in between; to act, or to do nothing. I believe that if we listen with the ears of our souls we can sometimes hear the voice of God saying, "If you choose to, you can _____." (We are free to fill in the blank with a choice drawn from the wide range of options for doing good that exist in our world.) We may not have the power to cure leprosy as Jesus did, but we do have power to make a difference in the world around us, usually in small ways, but sometimes in significant ways. It's up to us. It's our choice. We can decide to live our life for a purpose, or we can let ourselves drift along like a twig on a pond, pushed here or there by the winds of circumstance, not committing to any goals beyond securing food and shelter and pleasure for ourselves. A life lived without a higher purpose is a wasted life!

Liberty to make choices entails the possibility of making mistakes. We can exercise our freedom of choice—intending only to do something worthwhile, something positive, something good—and later learn that what we did resulted in consequences very different from what we had contemplated. Does that mean, then, that we should give up and remain inert because our well-intended actions might turn out badly, or not achieve all the good we'd intended? Of course not. If we choose what seems good and right, as God has given us grace to perceive it, then we trust God for the outcome.

Choice plays a major role in the life of faith. *Faith itself is a choice*. In my experience, faith is not a "zap" from above. We don't say, "Yesterday I didn't have faith, but I got 'zapped' this morning, and now I do." Faith is not a zap; it's a choice. I'm not discounting the role of the Holy Spirit in giving us a nudge in the right direction, but deciding to follow Jesus as our guide on life's journey and practice the Christian faith is a decision we freely make. It's a decision to look at ourselves, God, and other people from a particular angle—from the perspective offered by the gospel. But we're also at liberty to choose the perspective of godlessness, or even meaninglessness. Some philosophers believe human existence has no inherent meaning. We may buy into that. We're free to reject faith completely and regard ourselves and others as if we were actors in a pointless play—characters in a theater of the absurd.

Finding the Way

Thomas Aquinas is reputed to have said, "Every choice is a renunciation." To choose the perspective of faith requires the renunciation of other options. The life of faith is a life of choosing to trust God again and again, as long as we live, because "other options" will always present themselves to us, particularly in times of crisis. The life of faith is a matter of putting ourselves in God's hands daily, choosing to behave in ways consistent with our faith. Count on this: we *will* make mistakes. There are going to be occasions when we do things that seems good to us, only to see things turn out far differently from what we had expected. But faith tells us to trust God for the ultimate outcome and keep moving on. As Paul says, "We know that in all things God works for good for those who love God, who are called according to his purpose" (Rom 8:28, author's translation). Those who trust him will come to see that God is at work for good "in all things," including our mistakes.[2]

The most enduring questions in religion, philosophy, and psychology deal with the meaning of life. They are the great existential questions everyone faces at some point, either because of a brush with death, sudden reversal of fortune, heartbreak, disillusionment with life, arrival at a crossroads, a conversion experience, or simply through rigorous thinking. The questions may be formulated in different ways, but this list represents them succinctly:

- Who am I?
- What am I here for?
- How can I be happy?
- What should I do with my life?
- How do I make the right choices?
- Where do I belong?
- What is the point of striving when life is so short?

The answer to each of these questions calls for a personal choice, and the way each person arrives at an answer will be affected by the circumstances of that individual's life.

The most peaceful, fulfilled people I know have lives organized around and motivated by a single spiritual principle manifested in the gospel: *God*

2. The four preceding paragraphs have been revised from McNab, *Let Your Light Shine*, 51–52.

loves me, and therefore I am impelled to love God and my neighbor. Earlier in this book I suggested that God created us to receive his love; that this is our *raison d'être*.[3] That's the simplest answer to the age-old question, "What am I here for?" I'm here to receive the love of God and respond to that love with every choice I make during my life—as a child, as a student, as a friend, as a spouse, as a parent, as an employee, as a coworker, as a leader or a follower, as a retired person, and, finally, as an aging and dying person.

At every stage of my life I am free, within the physical and social limitations of each stage, to shape the responses I make to my experience of the love of God. As followers of Jesus grapple with the great existential questions, we do so within the context of lives defined and dignified by the love God pours on us as we persevere on the journey to which Christ has called us and upon which he is leading us. God's love evokes from us a responsive love—for God, for our brothers and sisters, and for the world. Out of our perception of divine love and our response to that love, we Christian pilgrims formulate our answers to the great existential questions.

It's important to distinguish between two questions: "What is the purpose of life?" (concerning universal, ultimate meaning) and "What should I do with *my* life?" (concerning our personal life goals, which vary from one of us to another and shift as we pass from childhood to maturity to old age). The two are related, of course, because spiritual integrity requires that our understanding of the purpose of human existence should directly affect the choices we make about what we do at every stage on our personal journey. Alan Jones says,

> Our full humanity, as men and women, is a journey, a movement, a calling.... Vocation implies a call from beyond, from the beyond that is within us all. Vocation, journeying, has an "I can do no other" quality about it and presupposes what Christians call grace. ... I did not ask to be born. Neither did I ask to be a priest.... Like birth, it is a gift and I am stuck with it. I have to work out my own salvation with fear and trembling within this context. There is my problem.... We live in an age when the fulfillment of the need of the moment is regarded as an inalienable right. Anything is permissible in the pursuit of what we pretentiously call our destiny. We sever relationships with casual brutality and ignore responsibility with self-righteous protestations.... In theological terms we affirm that a human being is made after the image of God. It is the mark of divinity which drives us mad and gives us

---

3. See, p. 38 above.

hope. It drives us mad because human life is open and unfinished. It gives us hope because life's openness is openness to God himself. This openness leaves us asking many questions. We have to learn to live with our problems and questions. Indeed we have to *live* the questions."[4]

Our journey with Jesus is a lifelong process of growth and change as we go forward with him in faith, and "faith is the foundation of our hope, the conviction of what we can't yet see" (my paraphrase of Heb 11:1). Persisting on that journey requires us to "live" the big existential questions even though we haven't resolved them all. The opposite of faith is not doubt or questioning, but certainty. We have faith, not certainty; but we do have Christ. And, as Alan Jones writes, "For Christians he is determinative. . . . Christ is, above all, the pilgrim, *the* pioneer. He is out there ahead of us, beyond and above all that we are, in all that we know of life."[5]

If our reason for being is to receive the love of God and respond to that love with every choice we make, then—logically—a "purposeful life" is going to be one in which we determine to incarnate that reason for being in all we do. Because God loves us, we're impelled to love God and our neighbors. If we happen to be young people who are still in school and haven't yet chosen a career path, we can live purposeful lives as students. And when we do choose a career path, we might discover one that is congruent with what we discern as God's purpose for our lives. The only options closed to us would be self-centered ones, focused exclusively on the acquisition of wealth, power, or status. In his best-selling book *The Purpose Driven Life*, Rick Warren writes, "Humility is not thinking less of yourself; it is thinking of yourself less. Humility is thinking more of others."[6] If we happen to be more mature adults when we start our journey with Jesus, perhaps already deeply invested in a career or even approaching retirement, there are still many ways we can choose to implement a newfound recognition of our purpose in life.

Another way of thinking about purpose is to understand it as our calling from God. Earlier, I quoted the words of Paul, in Romans: "In all things God works for the good of those who love him, *who have been called according to his purpose*" (Rom 8:28, italics added). Elsewhere he says, "I beg you to *lead a life worthy of the calling to which you have been called*, with all

---

4. Jones, *Journey*, 76–77.
5. Ibid., 78.
6. Warren, *Purpose*, 148.

Living with a Purpose

humility and gentleness, with patience, bearing with one another in love" (Eph 4:1–2 NRSV). The idea that each person who follows Christ is called by God has been part of Christian teaching from the beginning. In fact, secular use of the word "vocation" (from the Latin *vocare*, "call") to describe one's chosen trade or profession is borrowed from biblical descriptions of the calling of prophets and apostles to do God's work and proclaim his presence in the world.

By the middle ages, the idea of vocation came to be identified exclusively with religious leadership. Those who chose the path of ordained ministry in the church were expected to have a consciousness of being "called" by God to that work, whether through a mystical experience or in other ways, but secular work was not thought of in the same way. At the time of the Protestant Reformation, however, both Martin Luther and John Calvin expanded the traditional understanding of divine calling to include all Christians, not only those with religious vocations, since all are called to follow Christ in daily life. The reformers asserted that any work done for the glory of God and the benefit of others was a vocation from God. Calvin, in particular, taught that in spite of society's regard for some forms of work as more honorable than others, every kind of work has dignity and importance when it is a fulfillment of an individual's calling from God.[7]

Since God is purposeful in all God does and God is the source of human gifts and abilities, it's logical to believe that the gifts God has given each of us are meant to be used in fruitful and fulfilling ways, both for our own satisfaction and the good of others. When we respond to Christ's call to follow him on our life journey, we put our future in his hands and trust that he will guide us in making decisions about how to use our gifts.

Furthermore, in a spiritual sense, we ought not to assume that our vocation needs to be identical with our job. It may well be that our calling from God isn't one that society treats as a financially viable livelihood. And even if it is—such as an artistic vocation—there are many gifted musicians, painters, and sculptors who earn most of their income for years, sometimes for their whole life, from work unrelated to their art. In addition, both people who are unemployed and people who are retired continue to have vocations. Reformed theologian Nancy Duff writes, "Our lives have divinely

---

7. See Gregg, "Discover," 1–4.

ordained purpose where we are and who we are at any given moment."[8] Everyone who follows Christ has a vocation from God, and, with prayer and openness to inspiration, every Christian can ultimately identify and claim a purpose for his or her life.

There are well-known examples of people who have lived—and are living—purposeful lives. Johann Sebastian Bach was one of the most gifted musicians in history. From childhood he knew the purpose of his life was to create music, and he meant all of his music to be for the glory of God. On every musical manuscript Bach wrote, he inscribed "S.D.G." for the three words of the Latin phrase *Soli deo gloria*, "to God alone be the glory." Mother Teresa of Calcutta was a Roman Catholic nun and headmistress of a school until she received what she later described as "the call within the call," a deeply felt summons from God to leave the convent and give her life in ministry to the homeless poor while living among them. Paul Farmer is a brilliant anthropologist-physician and Harvard University professor who has dedicated himself to bringing health care to the poorest people on earth. He started virtually by himself with a clinic in Haiti, which he financed from his Harvard Medical School faculty salary by limiting the amount of money he spent on himself and living in one room of a church rectory. Quickly he enlisted friends, colleagues, and donors to share his vision, and moving outward from Haiti, Farmer's organization, Partners in Health, expanded first to South America and then to Africa. His work has gained international recognition.[9]

Very few of us are going to be like J. S. Bach or Mother Teresa or Dr. Paul Farmer. But all of us can be inspired by the example of their purposeful lives. Furthermore, we can all name people in our own circle of acquaintances who have a clear vision for their lives, a sense of purpose, and the deep awareness of a vocation from God. Our friends are probably not writing glorious music that will still be played in the year 2400 or caring for the homeless poor in the slums of a tropical metropolis or bringing medical care to the sick and dying citizens of the world's most impoverished nations. But we do have neighbors and family members who are dedicated to teaching children, volunteering at homeless shelters, planting community gardens, mentoring returning veterans, organizing choirs, comforting the

---

8. Duff, "Reformed," 311.

9. There are numerous biographies of J. S. Bach and many books about Mother Teresa. Tracy Kidder's 2003 book, *Mountains Beyond Mountains* is probably the best account of how Paul Farmer began his life's work.

dying, beautifying run-down neighborhoods, leading Bible studies, or doing any one of a thousand different other things that call for faith, love, selflessness, compassion, vision, and a deep concern for the wellbeing of others. Many of them understand that the undertaking which an insensitive bystander might discount as merely the pastime activity of a "do-gooder" is actually at the very center of their life's deep meaning. These friends of ours understand that a life without a higher purpose is a wasted life. But we don't arrive at recognition of our life's purpose simply by seeing the good things other people are doing and wishing we could be like them. We must be true to ourselves and aware of both our gifts and our limitations.

In his book *Let Your Life Speak*, Quaker educator and philosopher Parker J. Palmer writes about how he began to be seriously troubled by questions about his life vocation when he was in his thirties. He had finished a PhD and he had an interesting job, but he would wake up in the night and lie in bed worrying about his apparent lack of a meaningful vocation. His life appeared to be going well, but he was concerned that he was living a life guided merely by conventional American norms of success. He sensed a deeper, truer life hidden inside him, but he didn't know whether he could connect with it. Then,

> I ran across the old Quaker saying, "Let your life speak." I found those words encouraging, and I thought I understood what they meant: "Let the highest truths and values guide you. Live up to those demanding standards in everything you do." Because I had heroes at the time who seemed to be doing exactly that, this exhortation had incarnate meaning for me—it meant living a life like that of Martin Luther King, Jr. or Rosa Parks or Mahatma Gandhi or Dorothy Day, a life of higher purpose.
>
> So I lined up the loftiest ideals I could find and set out to achieve them. The results were rarely admirable, often laughable, and sometimes grotesque. But always they were unreal, a distortion of my true self—as must be the case when one lives from the outside in, not the inside out. I had simply found a "noble" way to live a life that was not my own, a life spent imitating heroes instead of listening to my heart.
>
> Today, some thirty years later, "Let your life speak" means something else to me, a meaning faithful both to the ambiguity of those words and to the complexity of my own experience: "Before you tell your life what you intend to do with it, listen for what it

intends to do with you. Before you tell your life what truths and values you have decided to live up to, let your life tell you what truths you embody, what values you represent."[10]

Palmer discovered that identifying our true calling comes through "listening to our life" and trying to understand what our life is really about—apart from what we would *like* for it to be about, if we could imitate our personal heroes. Unless we "let our life speak" to us, we are likely to block the expression of our own true significance. But letting our life speak also means letting it tell us some hard things we won't like to hear, and which we certainly don't intend to share with others. Palmer says, "My life is not only about my strengths and virtues; it is also about my liabilities and my limits, my trespasses and my shadow. An inevitable though often ignored dimension of the quest for 'wholeness' is that we must embrace what we dislike or find shameful about ourselves as well as what we are confident and proud of. That is why the poet says, 'ask me mistakes I have made.'"[11]

If we don't yet know what our divinely-given higher purpose is, how do we get to the point where we recognize it? Are there trail markers, arrows along the way that point toward our calling in life? Obviously, there are many goals, great and small, and many tasks that are set for us or that we set for ourselves that are not to be identified with our divine calling or purpose. These are simply things that society expects of us or that we need to do in order to provide a home, raise and educate our children, and be good citizens—in short, behavior that arises from our sense of duty. Examination of our particular life circumstances can open the door to a simple understanding of God's will and purpose for our life, at least for the present moment. For instance: A mother might say with conviction and truth that it is God's will for her to change her baby's soiled diaper and feed the child when it's hungry; a husband might feel certain that it is God's will for him to love his wife and seek to give her joy and gladness; and a university student might accept that it is God's will for him or her to work hard and fulfill the requirements of the courses being studied.[12]

---

10. Palmer, *Let Your Life*, 2–3.

11. Ibid., 6–7.

12. Jean-Pierre de Caussade (1671–1751) was a French Jesuit spiritual director and writer who would have been forgotten except for a little book entitled *Abandonment to Divine Providence*, first published 110 years after his death. Caussade encourages those

Living with a Purpose

Obviously, not every aspect of our life can speak so clearly to us, but duty speaks unmistakably—if we have ears to hear. But if we're trying to discern our divine vocation, there are ways to do so and arrows that can point the way forward. But first we need to be able to answer yes to two questions: "Do I want to know God's will and honor God with my life?" and "Do I want to serve others and help meet the needs of the world, not just take care of myself and my family?"

Having affirmed our desire to know and do God's will and our willingness to serve others, the next step in this process is self-examination, a close look at our spiritual experiences, current life situation, encounters with failure, felt needs, and our gifts and talents. Here are some questions we'll need to answer:

- How well do we know ourselves? Are we "listening to our life"?
- Where have we discerned that God was most at work in our life?
- What are the realities of our life: Are we married or single? Do we have children or other dependents? Are we seriously in debt? Do we have a health problem?
- What have we learned from our failures and frustrations?
- What are our passions, the things we care the most about, the things we yearn to do?
- What would we be doing with our life right now if money or other obligations were not an issue?
- What are our gifts and talents, particularly those that have been recognized by the people who know us best?
- Who or what inspires us the most?

This process of self-interrogation is not a formula that will automatically result in an easy definition of our purpose in life, though it will clear away some of the obstacles and bring us to the point of being ready to discern the goal of our quest. The truth is, however, that Christians who have a strong sense of calling from God arrive at that understanding in a variety of different ways; there's no single, dominant pattern. Some discern their vocation through facing difficult life situations. One younger friend of mine who has had a number of ups and downs in his working life and

---

who seek to know and do God's will to trust that God is making his will known to them in the simplest circumstances of what they might describe as their obvious duty. See Caussade, *Abandonment*, 21–58.

experienced economic setbacks as a small-scale entrepreneur during the Great Recession said, "My purpose is ever-unfolding and the interpretation of my own meaning has changed over time. I have come to the very question, 'What is my purpose,' through dealing with life's challenges. I believe that without challenges in life some people might never ponder the question, except in casual curiosity rather than true introspection. Through adversity I've learned that my *real* purpose has nothing to do with satisfying my own needs and wants. My real purpose is to form a relationship with Jesus based on trust and faith and to identify how I can use my life to benefit others."

This is a man whose life orientation has shifted over a period of years from simply seeking financial security and the trophies that go along with what our culture calls "success" (a fine house, nice cars, fancy vacations, and expensive toys) to a focus on finding ways, small or great, to be of service to others. Sure, he'd like to be debt free and not worried about money, but he has made a journey—one might even call it a pilgrimage—from obsessive self-concern to finding gladness in making himself available to God in service to others.

I have another friend who is CEO of a growing and successful international business with a global reputation for practicing a positive, people-centered way of dealing with employees and customers alike. He gave me a description of how he came to discern the purpose of his life by responding to the love of God. The process began in his thirties with a somewhat presumptuous conversation with his pastor. He found this clergyman to be a likeable, engaging, and approachable person, so in the comfort of that relationship he chose to tell him that even though he was a member of the church, he wasn't sure whether he believed in God or not. My friend was being profoundly honest, but the response that came from his priest challenged his perspective. His pastor said, "That's okay. The good news is that *God believes in you!*"

That dialogue occurred about the time of the birth of his youngest son, and the two events compelled this young head of a family-owned company to contemplate the awesome power of God's unconditional love, which he felt was being echoed in the feelings he had for his children. He told me, "All of a sudden I grasped God's love for me, and that made me understand I was supposed to live my life in response to that unconditional love. This transformative event in my thirties led me to develop a vision for a life of touching as many lives as possible, as positively as I could. . . . And it all began with understanding that life has purpose when we can accept that it's God's love for us that is the power!"

This man's sense of God's calling him to touch the lives of others as positively as possible has shaped all of his personal relationships and guided his business career, since he has embodied it in the leadership vision of his company. His is an example of how our discovery of God's purpose for our life can sometimes serendipitously combine with our way of earning a living.

Those of us who have felt called to ordained ministry in the church are generally more experienced in articulating our sense of vocation than lay people are because the church demands that we examine the question of our call repeatedly as we move through the stages of preparation that precede ordination. We are questioned about it by our sponsoring church pastors, by denominational commissions, by bishops or other supervising clergy, and by seminary professors. But even after we satisfy our professors, our bishops, and ourselves that we are truly called by God to ministry in the church and receive the laying on of hands in ordination, the larger question of our uniquely *personal* sense of vision and purpose as an ordained minister often remains open.

Recently an intellectual Episcopal priest friend described how she resolved her own struggle with vocation. Although baptized as an infant, she turned away from the church as a teenager and joined her skeptical father in the assessment that Christians were people who couldn't hack real life and needed a crutch. During her college years at an ivy league university she had what she called "an experience of grace" that led her to the Episcopal Church. She described her conversion as being first to the *church*—particularly its liturgy—and only afterward to Jesus (during the first Holy Week she ever took seriously). Seven years later, she was ordained and began to experience the ordained minister's typical, ongoing self-examination:

> During the process for ordination, and seminary, it was always a challenge to sort out what was my purpose. Was I serving the church, or was I serving the Lord? The two aren't always the same, especially in an institutional church, though there are moments when they *are* one and the same and those moments are beautiful. Through my

early years of priestly ministry I came to understand that wrestling with this dilemma itself is in fact an aspect of my purpose: wanting to follow Jesus, and doing so in the church, yet often being thwarted by the institutional church while at the same time recognizing it as the means by which many—including me—have been drawn to Jesus. I want to hold up Jesus to the church not only as Lord of all, but also as our humble, human goal and guide.[13]

I am persuaded that Jesus was and is the Son of God, and I am equally convinced that he lived among us as a fully human person. That's why he can be our guide and exemplar as well as our Savior. Those who assume Jesus had a completely articulated vision for his life from the time he was born are missing the clues in the four gospels that reveal a man whose sense of mission evolved, even during the three years of his ministry. Although early in those three years he seems to have had premonitions of a possible death at the hands of his enemies, he continued to proclaim the good news of the kingdom and teach the "higher righteousness" in parables and precepts, such as those we find in the Sermon on the Mount. Even as late as the night he was seized in the garden of Gethsemane, it apparently still seemed possible to Jesus that there might be an alternative to the cross.

If, indeed, coming to a full awareness of his Father's purpose and willingly yielding himself to it was a *process* in the life our Lord, there is no reason for us to expect the recognition of our own calling, and agreement to it, should be either quick or easy. On the spiritual journey, as Parker J. Palmer has pointed out, we discover a paradox: when a door closes, the rest of the world opens up. "The door that closed kept us from entering a room, but what now lies before us is the rest of reality."[14]

Coming to the point where we perceive and claim our life purpose, our vocation from God, will take time. Some doors will close, and others will open. It will demand self-examination, prayer, experimentation, and perhaps several changes of course. But the process is worth it.

---

13. This and the preceding two quotations are from personal friends who have chosen to remain anonymous.

14. Palmer, *Let Your Life*, 54.

Living with a Purpose

For Your Reflection

After reading chapter 7, "Living with a Purpose"

- When do you feel the most free and at liberty to make choices for your life? What do you think is the source of that feeling of freedom?

- When, if ever, do you feel the least free, the most inhibited, and not at liberty to make decisions for your life? What do you think is the source of that feeling of inhibition?

- In light of what you have learned and thought about as you have moved through this book, offer your answers to these three great existential questions:

    - Who am I?
    - What am I here for?
    - How can I be happy?

- Remember a time in your life, if there has been one, when you felt the most completely integrated as a person—that is, when your faith, your sense of higher purpose, your values, your work, and perhaps even your pastimes felt congruent, harmonious, and complementary to one another. If that is not your present situation, why isn't it? Is there a way to get back to that way of being?

- As you look back on your personal history, what have been the occasions when "doors closed" for you? After those doors closed, did others open? Was your life "speaking to you" then?

- Perhaps you are praying for a career that will be identical to your vocation from God, a profession that will blend both your sense of higher purpose and your way of earning a living. Consider these words of Frederick Buechner:

    > The kind of work God usually calls you to is the kind of work *(a)* that you need most to do and *(b)* that the world most needs to have done. If you really get a kick out of your work, you've presumably met requirement *(a)*, but if your work is writing TV deodorant commercials, the chances are you've missed requirement *(b)*. On the other hand, if your work is being a doctor in a leper colony,

Finding the Way

you have probably met requirement *(b)*, but if most of the time you're bored and depressed by it, the chances are you have not only bypassed *(a)* but probably aren't helping your patients much either. Neither the hair shirt nor the soft berth will do. The place God calls you to is the place where your deep gladness and the world's deep hunger meet.[15]

How might *you* go about finding that "place where your deep gladness and the world's deep hunger meet"?

- What are the trail markers or "arrows" along your life path that you see pointing towards your higher purpose?

---

15. Buechner, *Wishful Thinking*, 95.

Chapter 8

Finding a Church

Now when Jesus came into the district of Caesarea Philippi, he asked his disciples, "Who do people say that the Son of Man is?" And they said, "Some say John the Baptist, but others Elijah, and still others Jeremiah or one of the prophets." He said to them, "But who do you say that I am?" Simon Peter answered, "You are the Messiah, the Son of the living God." And Jesus answered him, "Blessed are you, Simon son of Jonah! For flesh and blood has not revealed this to you, but my Father in heaven. And I tell you, you are Peter, and on this rock I will build my church, and the gates of Hades will not prevail against it."

—MATTHEW 16:13–18 NRSV

THE UNITED STATES IS a nation of consumers. We like to shop; some people even think of shopping as a recreational activity, like golf or hiking. When they have a leisure afternoon, they like to go to the mall and wander from store to store. Even if they don't buy anything, they like to look at what's for sale and think about what they would buy if they had enough money. I tease my wife about being a "recreational shopper," and she doesn't deny it. I won't go on to discuss the world of online shopping, but I know millions of people spend countless hours web surfing in quest of new clothes, new computer hardware, new kitchen appliances, new cars, and sometimes even a new spouse. Everything anybody could possibly want—as well as a lot of things they shouldn't want—is being offered on the world wide web.

Most American churches welcome some worshipers every Sunday whom we unofficially describe as "church shoppers," people looking for a church. As a pastor who greeted visitors and newcomers at the church door

Finding the Way

for many years, I learned how to spot folks who were church shopping. Sometimes people would tell me they were church shoppers when they shook hands, but that didn't happen very often. Church shoppers usually want to remain anonymous, pretending they have just stopped at a random church to worship on Sunday the same way they might pull into a Shell station this week and an Exxon station next week to gas up the car. To identify church shoppers, most Protestant churches put cards in pew racks for visitors and newcomers to fill out and drop in the collection plate, if they are interested in learning more about the congregation. When people return a card, the pastor or someone else from the congregation usually contacts them to welcome them, either by a home visit, letter, or email.

No doubt many people do online church shopping before they show up on Sunday morning. Churches know that, so they post eye-catching websites, designed to appeal to people who are shopping for a church, with helpful links and pictures of happy people participating in parish activities. Websites are a form of church advertising. A website extols the church's strengths and virtues, all but promising church shoppers that if they attend Saint Mark's Episcopal (or Second Presbyterian or Trinity Lutheran) they will not only find God and grow in the Spirit, but also make new Christian friends, get help with parenting their troubled teenagers, enjoy interesting classes and recreational activities (such as church league softball, golf outings, or bowling in the parish rec center), and maybe participate in some worthwhile volunteer opportunities. "You can sign up for the annual young adults' mission trip. And don't forget, the Mardi Gras Ball is next week!"

Pastors and congregational leaders have learned a lot in the last few decades about marketing the church. Meanwhile, church shoppers have become sophisticated about how to read between the lines of church advertising. This all begs the question of whether churches ought to advertise. But we live in the United States, the world's foremost consumer nation, and the importance of advertising is rarely questioned.

When I go to a hardware store looking for a hinge to repair the gate in our back fence or an item of drapery hardware to keep the living room curtains from sagging, a store employee will usually find me roaming around and ask, "Are you finding what you're looking for?" Since I'm not a Mr. Fix-It who always knows exactly what item I *should* be looking for, I welcome the question. Usually I not only need to buy a hinge or some other stainless steel widget, I also need to buy a tool to help me install the thing. I may have several Greek lexicons and a bookcase of Bible commentaries, but I never seem to have the right sort of screwdriver or saw.

It occurs to me that in all my years as a pastor, functioning as a "church salesman," I was never bold enough to ask any church shoppers, "Are you finding what you're looking for?" That question, of course, would assume that they knew what they were seeking from a church. And that's no more certain with church shoppers than with all-thumbs clergy-types walking the aisles of Home Depot on Saturday afternoon. But both of us know we have urgent, unmet needs.

American churches behave in some ways like competitive businesses that are vying with one another for customers. The "consumerization" of our culture and the contemporary commodification of religion and spirituality have created an environment in which people who are seeking God are led to think of themselves as shoppers in a religious marketplace, where churches—along with other "vendors of spiritual goods and services"—are competing for their business. Church leaders have not intentionally chosen this model for congregational life, and many rue it as a mischaracterization, hoping to identify an alternative that depicts the relationship between local congregations in a less crass, commercial way. But the marketplace model seems to be the most accurate for understanding the current church scene in our country.

One of the downsides to the marketplace religious environment is that Christians who are church shopping while still uncertain about what they really need from the church sometimes approach their quest with habitual consumerist attitudes, and compare churches with one another on the basis of shallow, entertainment-oriented standards—such as the "star power" of the main preacher, the theatrical slickness of the worship service, music, and other media offerings, the physical characteristics of the church building, its aesthetics and amenities, and the number of educational and recreational programs offered. This is understandable, but guided only by such criteria, the process of looking for a church will simply sustain the consumer-driven status quo.

Not all church shoppers are consumerists of this sort, of course. There is a segment—usually younger adults—who regard as irrelevant or uninteresting the entertainment aspect of the worship services, the eloquence of

Finding the Way

the preaching pastor, and the variety of programs and small groups available in a prospective congregation. These seekers are after something else. They are consumer-driven, too, but their consumer standards are different. They intuitively know that *the church is the people*, not the building or the programs or the ecclesiastical apparatus, and they're trying to find a church made up of people who share their passions and who will welcome them as friends, even if they have unconventional theological opinions. And they have no commitment to the church as an institution. Blogger Christian Piatt, who represents this point of view, described his own search for a church this way:

> I wanted to find a group of people passionate about things that mattered to me, and who would make a space for me, regardless of whether we agreed on everything, or if I gave enough money, or if I had signed my name in some official book.
>
> For a lot of churches, that affirmation of belonging comes after you commit to membership as part of an institution. The problem for me was that I didn't really care about their institution; I only cared about the people. I came to understand the value of some institutions along the way, but young adults don't inherently trust institutions the way previous generations have, and we don't care nearly as much about preserving them either.
>
> Had my initial experiences with Christianity after my hiatus been with groups that had nice buildings and big budgets, I might not have stuck around. The fact that they had little to offer other than themselves was exactly what I was looking for.[1]

Church shopping is going to happen in one form or another, and serious church shoppers are entitled to guidance in how to assess whether a particular congregation is right for them. That's what I hope to offer in this chapter. Finding the right church is not like a visit to the hardware store. It's an extended process, not a quick decision based on a few facts and a little experience. Deciding whether to choose a particular church requires time, reflection, and prayer. If I continue with the shopping metaphor, I could say that the process of deciding on a church is like what buying a new car would be if a dealer were willing to let potential buyers drive a vehicle for a year or two before deciding whether they want to own it.

There are two ways of envisioning the church: first, as a heavenly ideal and, second, as a worldly reality. The heavenly ideal of the church is the kingdom of God, a cosmic and eternal part of God's plan for humanity. The

---

1. Piatt, "Four Reasons," n.p.

Finding a Church

earthly reality of the church is a collection of human institutions, shaped and reshaped by historical circumstances, a fragmented reflection and anticipation of that kingdom. These are not competing visions; they are complementary, but there is a tension between them.

The heavenly ideal of the church is grounded in the New Testament, which offers the vision of a kingdom that believers enter and begin to experience in this mortal life after they believe the gospel and trust their lives to Christ, but that they come fully to enjoy only in the life to come. In this vision, the church is the family of God, and the New Testament tells us that every human being is potentially a member of that family.

It is the worldly perception of the church, however, not the heavenly ideal, that dominates our thinking and behavior. In the worldly view, the church is a human social and religious institution striving to represent the heavenly ideal as best it can. In the context of world civilization, the church is identified with Christianity as a religion. To be a Christian is to be, at least nominally, a member of the church—and there are many churches (denominations), many different communities of believers, some very large and some very small, competing with various degrees of intensity for the allegiance of individual Christians. It is quite conceivable that within a hundred years there will be many fewer different Christian denominations than there are at present. But for now, denominationalism remains a Protestant reality.[2]

Why should someone who is making a personal commitment to follow Jesus bother with finding and associating with a local church? Could it not be sufficient to recognize that all followers of Jesus are part of the invisible, universal church, the mystical, worldwide body of Christ? Serious Christians have asked me, "Why do I need to belong to a church? Is it really necessary?" I have to stifle my defensive reflexes when I hear these queries, since I've spent my life serving Christ in the institutional church. But could the church as I've known it now be more a bane than a blessing? Is institutionalized Christianity on the way out? Are Americans now abandoning churches the way Europeans seem to have done back in the 1960s?

Diana Butler Bass says Americans are living through a "Great Religious Recession," what she describes as a "religious bear market," when not

---

2. For a short discussion regarding the future of denominationalism, see Lose, "Do Christian Denominations," n.p.

only the old mainline, liberal Protestant denominations are declining, but conservative evangelical ones, as well. Bass offers examples of Protestants and Catholics who have decided to be "spiritual, but not religious." These people still identify with Jesus, but not with what they call "religion."[3] Such individuals may well be spiritual seekers, but they are not going to be church shoppers—at least not now. In addition, the Pew Research Center reports that one-fifth of the US public and one-third of adults under thirty identified themselves as religiously "unaffiliated" in 2012, and those numbers increased very rapidly in the five years leading up to 2012.[4]

In some respects, the institutional church appears to create more problems than it provides value, especially in the eyes of new or newly recommitted Christians, those whom I identify as returnees or restarts. They love Jesus. They want to follow Jesus and repudiate the me-centered mindset of contemporary society. They want to live their faith. They want to reflect on the Bible, share the love of the Father, worship, pray, and love their neighbors as themselves. But they do not want to identify with a big, corporate organization. When they look at the traditional, institutional church they tend to see only its shadow side—its sins, shortcomings, failures, divisions, and loss of missional focus. If they are going to decide to become part of a local church, they want it to be one that feels right for them, and especially one that practices what it preaches.

A friend said to me not long ago, "I feel more inspired by the men's Bible study group I belong to and closer to them than I ever feel in church on Sunday. Why can't my Bible study group be 'church' enough for me?" A cradle Episcopalian, he added, "Except for Holy Communion, what more do I need?" People whose lives have been changed by Alcoholics Anonymous say similar things about AA. They ask why the church can't be more like AA. They never miss attending its meetings, whether they're at home or traveling. They wonder why they don't feel as dependent on the church. Alcoholics Anonymous has the peculiar virtue of being a racially, socially, culturally, and economically diverse group of people, all of whom recognize their shared besetting sin. (That description would have fit the New Testament church.) Rich or poor, college graduates or high school dropouts, all

---

3. Bass, *Christianity*, 11–26. Chapter 5 of this book, "Behaving," is an excellent explanation of Christianity primarily as a way of life, rather than a system of doctrine.

4. Pew Research Center, "Nones," 9.

Finding a Church

AA members recognize themselves as fallible, weak, broken, and addicted. They're in touch with their most dire needs. AA is their lifeboat, and they're eager to haul in anybody else who's drowning. They want to help. It's easy for churches to lose sight of the fact that they, too, are meant to be lifeboats.

The people I mentioned raise legitimate questions about the nature of Christian community, and they're entitled to know what a local church should be like and what it should be able to do. They aren't disputing that Jesus wanted to establish a closely-knit community of disciples rather than merely attract random individual admirers. But they want to know, "Did Jesus intend his church to look like *this*?" That's a good question, and the answer is "Probably not." But if we believe in the loving providence of God and God's ability to achieve his ultimate purposes in spite of human error and sin, then we have to believe that God is working through those frail, flawed, and fragmented—but well-intentioned—worldly embodiments of his kingdom that we know as churches. All human institutions are flawed—political, educational, scientific, charitable, and religious institutions alike. But all human institutions can ultimately be reformed. Seekers who have not abandoned religion in favor of a purely private spirituality and who hope to find a local church must be prepared to settle for one that is less than perfect. But they are entitled to some clear standards by which to evaluate the churches they might decide to visit.

I contend that people who want to be numbered among the disciples of Jesus Christ *need to find a church*. For disciples, the church is not an optional extra we may choose or dispense with, as each of us feels inclined. Church is necessary to the life of Christians. Participating in a neighborhood Bible study or a prayer group is good, but will not provide breadth of vision, and worshiping first at one church and then another cannot provide the rootedness Christians need in order to grow. The First Letter of Peter identifies the local church as a fellowship, a "brotherhood" (1 Pet 2:17), which I compare at the end of this chapter to a family.[5] Gordon T. Smith writes that *conversion*—the transformation from self-centeredness to Christ-centeredness—is "a complex experience by which a person is initiated into a common life with the people of God who together seek

---

5. The New Testament Greek word *adelphotēs*, used in 1 Pet 2:19 and usually translated "brotherhood," does not exclude sisters. In Greek, the words for brother and sister are identical except for masculine or feminine suffixes.

the in-breaking of the kingdom, both in this life and in the world to come. This experience is mediated by the church and thus necessarily includes Baptism as a rite of initiation. The power or energy of this experience is one of immediate encounter with the risen Christ—rather than principles or laws—and this experience is choreographed by the Spirit rather than evangelistic techniques."[6]

Bishop Lesslie Newbigin, who spent most of his life in India bringing different Christian denominations together and working among people who were coming to Christianity from Hinduism or Islam, argued that conversion is a matter of three things: (1) *understanding*, (2) *ethics*, and (3) *community*. That is to say, individuals cannot experience conversion to Christ without transformation of the intellect, submission to the lordship of Christ in their moral life, and incorporation into a faith community marked and sustained by its Christ-centered, gracious sacramental experiences of Baptism and Eucharist. "Newbigin's fundamental observation and conviction is that the church is not a provider of religious products and services but rather that the church is a people in mission"[7] —a community of people who are a this-worldly embodiment of the heavenly kingdom.

The church is the *people*, the family of God—the body of Christ, as Paul labeled it (1 Cor 12:27). No serious Christian doubts this. Although the church might be a social institution, as formally defined, the church is not to be identified with any given set of institutional or organizational structures. The various churches—Roman Catholic, Orthodox, Anglican, and Protestant—all have their own differing organizational structures, traditions, and rules, some of which are elaborate and others quite simple. But all these denominations would agree that the church is the *holy people of God*—not the hierarchy, not the properties, not the worship forms, not the organizational rules. All such structures are dispensable.

The only thing truly essential for the church is the living presence of Jesus himself within the community of disciples, and this presence is mediated and experienced in a variety of ways. Jesus says, "Where two or three are gathered in my name, there am I in the midst of them" (Matt 18:20). The church by definition is the body of disciples called together by Jesus and centered on him, a worldwide communion scattered among millions

---

6. Smith, "New Conversion," n.p.
7. Ibid., 2.

of local congregations. Church is all about Jesus. The church was born beside the Sea of Galilee on that day when Jesus first called four fishermen to leave their boats and nets and follow him. Those first four disciples were the nucleus of the church.

When Paul says the church is the body of Christ, he's telling us that he sees even a relatively small, local community of disciples as an organic extension of the incarnation. By being part of the church, each disciple is mystically united with Christ—and with all other Christians. In 1 Corinthians 12:11–28, Paul offers his now-familiar analogy of the body, comparing the members of the church to the various limbs and organs of the body of Christ himself. Since the beginning, Christians have understood sharing Holy Communion as a mystical and sacramental renewal of our identification with Christ and with one another.

Despite all this, many Americans still find it easy to see churches merely as worldly, dispensable institutions. Think about how people usually ask one another about their association with the church. The most common way is to ask, "Where do you *go to church*?" This is similar to asking a child, "Where do you *go to school*?" It calls for an institutional, even geographic, answer. But "going to church" does not mean exactly the same thing as being part of the body of Christ. We know that instinctively. Being a churchgoer, or even a church member, is not the same as being a *disciple*, in the same way that being a "school-goer" (i.e., sitting in a classroom) is not the same as being a serious student. Though ideally there should be no distinction between being a church member and being a disciple, we know many people whose names are on church rolls but who have no meaningful relationship with Christ.

Although we might regret the common identification of the church with a building—a house of worship—it's important to recognize that the idea of the holy place is deeply embedded in the human psyche. Human beings have been identifying certain sites as sacred since prehistoric times, and it's a practice we can presume will continue far into the future. The fact that Christians now possess easily identified houses of worship can be seen as an asset, not just as an unfortunate institutional encumbrance. For example, church buildings provide obvious venues to which church returnees can come and to which inquirers can go to learn about the way of Jesus. Neither returning to church after a season away nor finding a group of Christians who could tell a faith-seeker about Jesus would be easy if Christians gathered only in unidentified places at random times.

Finding the Way

The book of Acts and the letters of Paul offer insights into the ordinary life of the earliest Christian communities. One thing stands out about these churches: in the earliest days of Christianity, local congregations were usually small enough to gather in a home.[8] Members of each church knew one another and felt called to love one another. At times this love proved false; at times there were factions that formed around different teachers; at times there were divisions on the basis of wealth or social station. But it was always expected that within these communities there would be mutual support, interdependence, and accountability. Members were urged to have "the mind of Christ," and the members of one local church knew and shared concern for the members of the other local churches, recognizing the essential unity they shared. Nevertheless, there were also conflicts and disagreements; the saints who sat at the feet of Peter and Paul were as imperfect as we are.

Acts 2:41–45 says that the early church in Jerusalem just after the Day of Pentecost "had all things in common" and that the charity of the church met the needs of all the poor disciples. That experiment appears not to have been imitated anywhere else, however. There were diversities of gifts and ministries in each local congregation, and there was nothing resembling our present professional ordained ministry. The early churches were quite charismatic in every sense of the word, each one shaping its life according to the evident giftedness of those who made up the local body.

We should be careful not to romanticize those New Testament churches. They were not composed of social friends; they were in no sense "religious clubs." Paul's two letters to the church in Corinth make it apparent that the Corinthian Christian community had serious problems. First-century believers were not morally superior to twenty-first-century believers, but none in that period were merely "nominal church members" of the type we recognize today. Such a category did not yet exist. Most seem to have been serious about following Jesus faithfully. Some had given up a great deal for the sake of their new faith, and many were prepared to face

---

8. Before the clear separation between Christians and Jews (which happened about the time of the destruction of the Jerusalem Temple by the Romans in AD 70), Christians were a sect within Judaism and probably dominated certain synagogues, particularly in Judea. After Church and Synagogue split, Christians seem to have assembled for worship in homes. Typically, in the New Testament era there was only one church in any given city. There is no evidence that there was any effort to keep the identity of Christian gathering places was secret until after official persecution began, late in the first century.

Finding a Church

death rather than deny Christ. They were also submitted to the teaching and leadership of the apostles, though there continued to be factional disputes about which apostles were "greater."[9] The gospels show us that during Jesus' ministry, he had to reprimand the Twelve for disputing among themselves about which one of them had best reason to claim top rank. That debate seems to have continued after Pentecost, despite Jesus' earlier rebuke. And it's still going on.

Matthew's gospel suggests that Jesus expected the community of his followers would be small, relative to the societies in which they were placed. In parables, he compares his followers to "salt," "light," and "yeast" (Matt 5:11–15; 13:33). A pinch of salt adds flavor to a dish; a single oil lamp drives away the darkness in a room; a little leaven causes a whole loaf of dough to rise. If Christ assumed that the various communities of his followers would be small relative to the societies in which they were set yet provide the out-of-proportion impact of a pinch of salt, a single flame, or a bit of yeast, this tells us he expects the presence of his followers, even though few in number, to make a decisive difference in the societies around them.

History shows that those first tiny communities of disciples fulfilled their Lord's expectations, and did so by exercising what James Davison Hunter calls a "ministry of faithful presence," a life together in which they were fully present in loving service, equally to one another *and* to those outside the Christian community. As Hunter uses the expression, "faithful presence" means Christians' imitation of God, our creator and redeemer, by identifying with others in the same way the incarnate Son of God identified with sinful humanity, directing our lives towards the flourishing of others through sacrificial love.[10] This ministry of faithful presence in the world implements Christ's command to love our neighbors as ourselves. The first small church communities demonstrated the love of God for *all* people. Christians have a mission to make disciples (Matt 28:19), but also a mission to serve the welfare of the world, including the unconverted.

If people trying to find a church don't want to behave as merely shoppers in a religious marketplace, there are certain aspects of congregational life which they should evaluate during the extended process of deciding what congregation to choose. Because every disciple is unique and each

---

9. Illustrations of these particular characteristics of local churches can be found in various degrees of detail in the book of Acts and in Paul's Epistles, particularly 1 and 2 Corinthians.

10. Hunter, *To Change*, 244.

one's family circumstances vary, I would not presume to propose a comprehensive set of standards by which all seekers might compare one church with another. However, practical matters should never be overlooked and probably should be considered first. For example, families with children might want to find a church where their children's spiritual needs will be addressed appropriately and where families have opportunities to worship together in ways meaningful to both the adults and the children. Persons who have physical disabilities, such as hearing impairment or difficulty walking, will want to consider whether a particular congregation's facilities will prove practical for them over the long term. Proximity is not a decisive concern, but choosing a church located twenty miles from home might be problematic for many people and limit their ability to participate in the ongoing life of that congregation.

Beyond practical concerns, there are a variety of theological or doctrinal considerations, such as what a prospective church expects as a minimum statement of Christian belief from its members. Some churches are quite strict about doctrine and have a theological litmus test for prospective members, while others are very relaxed. Most American churches profess the Christian faith in terms of the Apostles' Creed, even if they don't employ the actual words of the ancient creed itself, while others have their own unique, specific doctrinal declarations and require members to subscribe to them. By contrast, there are a few denominations and many independent churches that tolerate a broad range of theological views from both pastors and members, proposing few or no doctrinal norms. All churches teach that God speaks both to the church and to individuals through the Bible. Many understand the Bible as the work of people who were inspired by the Holy Spirit, but who wrote within the context of their cultures and chose their own vocabulary for communicating divine truth, while others insist that the Bible is a harmonious and unified book whose words (at least in the original languages) were dictated by God himself. Nearly all churches administer the sacraments of Baptism and the Eucharist, though the particulars of how the sacramental rites are described, understood, and performed will differ from church to church.[11]

---

11. Protestants in general understand that a "true" church is one where "the gospel is rightly preached and the sacraments rightly administered." This of course begs the question of what constitutes right preaching and right administration. About what is "right" there is a wide difference of opinion between churches. This is why there are about thirty-eight thousand different Christian denominations today.

Regardless of denominational identity, there are at least five spiritual criteria important to consider in the quest to find the "right" church. Being guided by these criteria will preclude choosing to become part of a church purely on the basis of what it might provide for us as religious consumers.

First and most importantly, find a church that is *explicitly Christ-centered*. People who have taken Jesus as guide on life's journey, dedicating themselves to obey Christ as Lord and worship him as God incarnate, will not be satisfied with a church that fails to take the heart of the gospel seriously. Jesus is the heart of the gospel.

Second, look for a *teaching* church, where many opportunities are offered for members to learn and grow in faith and in understanding of how to make practical connections between faith and daily life. Parents should look for a church that provides opportunities for them to learn how to share their faith effectively with their children. A teaching church will take Scripture seriously and will invite its members to go deeper through a process of lifelong learning. An effective teaching church will be able to hold doubt and faithfulness in tension, welcoming hard questions while still pressing on toward answers. Learning situations need not always be in the form of structured instruction. The gospels show us that Jesus was always teaching—by example as often as by precept—and his followers were always learning. Discipleship is about becoming more and more like Jesus. No one is ever so advanced in the Christian life that there is not something more to learn about how to do that. Discipleship is not about giving the "right" answers to test questions.

Third, find a church that has *high expectations of its members*, both in terms of their engagement in service and in the moral order of their lives. Jesus told his disciples that he had come "not to be served, but to serve" (Mark 10:45). If we are faithful to our call to imitate Christ, then we will want to be part of a congregation that expects us to serve rather than wait to *be* served. Jesus summons us to be givers rather than receivers, and active doers of good works rather than passive observers of works being done by others (Matt 5:16). Seeking to become like Jesus entails ordering our moral lives by the standards of the gospel of Christ. That's part of what it means to live in the kingdom of God. It's important for church seekers to find a congregation prepared to offer practical help in the process of discerning good choices from bad ones. Because we do not live in a simple, black-and-white moral universe, we need a community of faith that will help us steer our path through the many difficult decisions and ambiguities of life in the twenty-first century. Our moral formation as disciples of Christ is inseparable from our spiritual formation and calls us out of self-centeredness into love for others.

Fourth, look for a church that *demonstrates active care for every member*—a church that shepherds each member, helps each member stay faithful, and equips all its members to shepherd one another. Although we do not affiliate with a church only to be passive receivers of ministry, we all have personal needs. From time to time we feel battered or weary or emotionally wrung out, and when we feel that way we want to have a community that will help us and love us. The gospels portray Jesus as the Good Shepherd who patiently tends his flock (Mark 6:34; John 10:1–16). He said, "Come to me, all you that are weary and are carrying heavy burdens and I will give you rest" (Matt 11:28 NRSV). Most churches would like to offer nurturing and healing help to members and non-members alike, but some do this more effectively than others—and in the most effective pastoral congregations, the shepherds who do the caregiving are as likely to be lay people as they are to be clergy. In such communities, the presumption is always that those who have been weak will grow strong again, those who have been sick will become healthy, and those who have been emotionally distraught will be restored to a peaceful mind. Often, members who have been loved and cared for by their church are the ones most motivated to love and care for others. In addition, we need the encouragement and examples of fellow disciples if we're to stay faithful to our journey with Jesus. There is a constant pressure to conform to the materialistic, consumeristic, entertainment-driven, me-centered society that surrounds us. Serious Christians are a counterculture in America and Europe today, and it's difficult to live according to that countercultural model unless we're members of a cohesive, nurturing community. We need brothers and sisters who share our faith, our values, and our way of life. The formalities of official, institutional church membership are less important—particularly to young adults—than is having the feeling that they "belong."

Fifth and finally, seek a church *with a mature and tested pastor and lay leaders*. Those who feel ready to become part of a local church need to evaluate and compare the leadership models and styles observable in the churches they are considering. In healthy congregations, tasks of leadership will be shared between the pastor and lay leaders. Nevertheless, in practice, the pastor of a church is its most visible representative. The pastor is the usual spokesperson for the church on Sundays and is the individual a seeker will most want to get to know before deciding whether to affiliate with a particular congregation. Anyone considering making a commitment to a church should spend time one-on-one with its pastor and should do so on more than one occasion. Make an appointment and have a serious talk. Ask questions. Then go back and visit again. If the pastor teaches a class, sit in on that class a few times. Keep in mind that pastors vary from one to another in their talents; multi-gifted, omni-competent pastors are not the rule. I have known some, but they aren't the norm. (I'm not one.) Some pastors are excellent preachers, but poor counselors. Others are gifted shepherds of their flock, but weak teachers. Still others have a knack for keeping the machinery of parish life running smoothly and efficiently, but prove disappointing in the pulpit.

Spiritual maturity and age do not always go hand-in-hand. Some younger pastors are wise beyond their years, while some older pastors seem to have learned little from their experience. A mature pastor will have learned how to listen to the Holy Spirit and articulate God's vision for the congregation. Such a pastor is comfortable saying to the church, "This is what I believe God wants us to do." Leaders must be accountable for their leadership. Pastors need to be working under a higher church authority, whether it's a bishop or a presbytery or a council of elders or a local church board. A pastor who is accountable only to God is dangerous. Pastors need to be held accountable, and they need to hold accountable those who serve under them.

Character is a more important quality in a pastor than so-called professional skills. A good pastor will be prayerful, humble, honest, forthright, wise, compassionate, approachable, good-humored, and teachable. He or she doesn't need to walk on water or work miracles or have all the right answers, but should always be a good listener. Discerning anyone's character takes time, but many subtle clues to character can be discerned by those who are observant. Keep in mind, however, that none of us is without faults, including those who have dedicated themselves to pastoral ministry.

Although people starting to look for a church might suppose the process of choosing one will be as simple, objective, and detached as shopping for a dress or buying a car, they will soon discover that it isn't. It may even seem that a certain congregation is "choosing us" rather than the other way around. By this I mean that our spiritual friends often shape our choice of a church. People with whom we have been sharing our journey with Jesus—to whom we have opened our hearts, with whom we have prayed for guidance, and who have loved us and helped us—have already linked their lives with ours in Christ. If the majority of our Christian friends are part of one particular congregation, their church will have a natural attraction for us. And that's a good thing.

If none of those with whom we've been sharing our spiritual journey have a church to which they are committed, then it might be a good idea to agree to look for a church together. Having partners in this prayerful search is an asset. But it will *not* be a good idea for our small group of Christian friends to decide to become our own private church, meet for worship regularly in one of our homes, and dispense with finding a larger body with whom to share a life together in Christ. If we choose that route, we will become a religious club, not a church. It is good for Christians to be participants in small, intimate fellowship groups—like Bible study groups, prayer groups, and affinity groups. In such small groups, an individual finds inspiration, meets peers who can function as examples, and is supported by the intercession of friends. Healthy congregations will include a number of such groups within their community life, but these groups are a subset of the church, not a substitute for it. Churches must encompass a wider diversity of people than any small group can, and churches must include people who are not like us but are bonded with us in one body through the work of the Spirit, rather than through ordinary human affections and affinities.

Since the universal church is the family of God in the ideal, or "heavenly," sense, then in the practical, or "worldly," sense, every local congregation should be more like an extended family than a club. Families are composed of people who acknowledge their kinship and their essential bond, even if they don't necessarily always like one another. The familial metaphor for the church has been criticized because we are born into a biological family, and those families are not open to new members the same way churches are. There's some truth in this criticism, but Jesus' image for our relationship with God is as his children, born "by water and the Spirit" (John 3:1–7). If we are God's children, then we belong to God's family. The New Testament consistently refers to fellow Christians, fellow members of the church, as brothers and sisters.

Finding a Church

It's essential for us to discard all models for being church that present it as merely a voluntary association like the Rotary Club or Friends of the Earth. A state might regard churches as voluntary associations according to its laws, but the New Testament says the church is a family, and membership in a family is not voluntary. We have the mothers and fathers and sisters and brothers that human kinship has given us. Thus, using family as the operative image for the church is profoundly important. The church is a worldwide family, not a worldwide association of like-minded and well-meaning people drawn together in millions of local units simply because they take pleasure in one another's company and share a common interest in, say, civic endeavors or environmentalism. Using *family* not just as a way of thinking about the universal church but as the primary metaphor for relationships within a local congregation reminds us that we are called by God to love and care for people in our immediate fellowship with whom we are not totally compatible, whose personal habits and interests are often dissimilar to our own, and with whom—under ordinary circumstances—we would probably not be social friends.

Think about your own family. If you have adult siblings, your sister might be your best friend—but she also might not be. You might not seek her out to be your weekly bridge partner or to go with you to Hawaii. Nevertheless, she will always be your sister. Every Thanksgiving, when you gather at your grandparents' house with your extended family, she will be there at the table. If there's a crisis in her life or yours, or if there's happy news to share, you will get in touch with one another right away. She will probably be among the first people you call. And unless there has been some tragic, awful impairment of your personal relationship, you will always be prepared to help your sister, listen to her woes, and, yes, *love* your sister, even though she may not be your best friend. And she will do the same for you.

Being part of a church community that includes close friends but also many who are not our chosen social companions puts us in the place of learning how to treat one another as brothers and sisters in Christ. This is not an easy lesson to learn. That's why some churches feel cold while others feel clubby. Neither sort makes us feel we belong.

Church should be like Grandma's house at Thanksgiving. The menu might always be pretty much the same, and Grandma's cornbread stuffing has never been our favorite dish, but it feels good and right to be there at her table for this feast. We might not have been with our sisters and brothers and cousins since last year at this time, but when we're all sitting at the table, there's no doubt about whether we belong together. All of us know the old family stories, but we still laugh at the punch lines despite having heard those yarns a thousand times. And every single one of us bears some aspect of the family likeness, whether it's the shape of our nose or our enjoyment of board games. This Thanksgiving, like most we can remember, Uncle Teddy will probably drink too much and Aunt Eunice will shirk her share of the clean-up duties. Nevertheless, those with us at the table are our family, and we love them.

Brothers and sisters, this is the church!

Finding a Church

For Your Reflection

After reading chapter 8, "Finding a Church"

If you are seeking to make a new start in your journey with Jesus but want to break with the currently dominant consumer-oriented model for envisioning the church before deciding what congregation to join, ask yourself the questions below. The answers you give to these questions will reveal truths about your spiritual experience, what you value most, how you think about your fellow Christians, and what you need most if you're to continue growing as a disciple of Christ. Answering these questions in advance will help church shoppers give a thoughtful answer to anyone who asks, "Have you found what you're looking for?"

- What experiences have brought me to a fresh decision to follow Jesus and look for a (new) church?
- What have I learned from those experiences about God, myself, and other people?
- How has God been speaking to me, guiding me, and showing me his will for my life?
- At this point on my journey, how do I recognize my own sin and how do I practice repentance and amendment of life?
- Do I discern the spiritual gifts and practical talents with which God has blessed me, or do I need more help with that?
- What people have helped me most on my journey thus far? How did I meet these people?
- Do I see myself in the "front lines" of service in years ahead or do I see myself more as helping to "support and supply" those who are in the front lines?
- What have been my most meaningful experiences with other Christians?
- What do I need to have in common with the other people in my (new) church?

Finding the Way

- Do I want to think about my fellow church members the same way I think about other loyal alumni of my college? Or do I want to think about them the same way I think about my sisters and brothers?
- What am I looking for from a church?
- What can I offer my (new) church community?

Chapter 9

Putting It All Together: Christianity as a Way of Life

You are a chosen race, a royal priesthood, a holy nation, God's own people, in order that you may proclaim the mighty acts of him who called you out of darkness into his marvelous light. Once you were not a people, but now you are God's people; once you had not received mercy, but now you have received mercy. Beloved, I urge you as aliens and exiles to abstain from the desires of the flesh that wage war against the soul. Conduct yourselves honorably among the Gentiles, so that, though they malign you as evildoers, they may see your honorable deeds and glorify God when he comes to judge. . . . For it is God's will that by doing right you should silence the ignorance of the foolish. As servants of God, live as free people, yet do not use your freedom as a pretext for evil. Honor everyone. Love the family of believers. Fear God. Honor the emperor.

—1 PETER 2:9–12, 15–17 NRSV

IN THE PREFACE TO this book, I write that my intent is to give practical help to people hungry for a personal relationship with God and for a living faith they might understand clearly, explain simply, practice faithfully, and share with their children and friends. I say that I want to inspire readers to make themselves progressively more available to God through obedience to Christ, and in so doing to discover that Christianity is a way of life, not just a set of doctrines. In this final chapter, I want to draw together the themes I have already addressed and make a final case for understanding Christianity as a way of life.

Finding the Way

Christianity has never presented itself as a system of belief, exclusive of behavior; nor have eastern religions, such as Buddhism, offered only a pattern of behavior, detached from foundational beliefs about humanity, life and death, the universe, and the divine. History does not tell us about any way of life that was independent from a system of ideas. Believers of all sorts put their beliefs into practice. And the practice of those beliefs is evident not just in the formal rites of church, synagogue, temple, or mosque, but in community life, family life, and personal behavior. This is why an anthropologist can observe life in a rural village in south India for a period of months and conclude from the accumulated data that its residents are Hindu, Muslim, or Christian based on their observable way of life.

A lifestyle *not* derived from a particular religious worldview or from a prescriptive traditional culture or from a school of philosophy will not be a "way of life" at all, but rather a shapeless and situational existence, moved from day to day only by the shifting trends of the prevalent culture, coupled with the individual's transitory appetites, ideas, and emotions. Unless shaped by a belief system and the way of life arising from it, the animal side of human nature—rather than the spiritual—is certain to dominate, and the result will be a life characterized by self-centeredness, opportunism, and pursuit of pleasure as an end in itself. (Perhaps unguided, spiritually rootless, pleasure-focused behavior will come to be identified as the twenty-first century's secular way of life.)

Human life is complicated. There is no society made up entirely of perfectly integrated human beings, all of whose actions are guided by deeply held convictions. Even people who usually practice a certain religious way of life—Christian or Hindu or something else—do not *invariably* behave in ways consistent with their beliefs. Christians' behavior may be guided *most of the time* by our profound convictions (such as trust in Christ and love of neighbor); but sometimes our behavior is contrary to our religious profession and way of life—motivated only by ambition, expediency, or lust. All of us are capable of professing certain faith convictions and moral values, being active members of a church, and living mostly Christian lives—while nevertheless making some of our choices only on the basis of what appears to be our immediate personal advantage. This means most of us who are Christians will sometimes fail to practice what we profess to believe. To put it simply, we all turn out to be hypocrites occasionally. But so do Buddhists,

Hindus, Muslims, Jews, and everyone else. All human beings sometimes fall short of their noblest ideals and find themselves behaving in ways that embarrass them. When that happens to us, it doesn't mean we've jettisoned our value system; it simply means we're human. In biblical terms, we're sinners. However, our goal is to learn how to practice a rule of life that maximizes the probability that we will behave as often as possible in ways consistent with the convictions of our faith, following in the footsteps of Jesus Christ.

Life would be easier if absolute certainty and moral clarity were always available, but many situations we encounter are fraught with ambiguity. Some choices seem black and white, but most are not so simple. Christian convictions will not automatically lead us to a better moral life than any other religion or philosophy can. After all, some form of the golden rule is found in the literature of many different faiths. Other religions and philosophies can also shape decent, ethically rigorous, and honorable lives. Following Jesus is not going to make Christians morally superior to other people. But following Jesus in faith with obedience and self-discipline will result in a consistent pattern of behavior, a *way of life* that

- keeps us mindful of God's love
- links us to a community of sisters and brothers who will support us
- gives meaning and purpose to our existence
- teaches us to practice gratitude and generosity
- offers a way of understanding our place in the universe
- empowers us to live in peace with the world around us, and
- shapes us to face the future in hope, despite our weaknesses, failures, and frustrations.

The Christian way of life equips us to endure the worst heartbreaks, tragedies, and ills of mortal existence, not merely with stoic calm, but with love, joy, peace, patience, kindness, generosity, faithfulness, gentleness, and self-control (Gal 5:23 NRSV).

American Christianity seems to have lost its grip on the biblical truth that following Christ is a *way of life* in faithful relationship to God and loving service to others, not just a system of doctrine.[1] In contemporary

---

1. See Bass, *Christianity*, 149. According to Bass, "Although Western Christianity would eventually be defined as a belief system about God, throughout its first five centuries people understood it primarily as spiritual practices that offered a meaningful way

Finding the Way

American culture, some church members' day-to-day life choices have become disconnected from their very careful statements of faith. This is probably why a statistically significant percentage of the American population self-identifies as Christian, although their way of living is obviously different from the way Christians lived in the apostolic age or even a hundred years ago.[2] Self-identified Christians today appear willing to compromise traditional Christian principles of behavior more readily than did their ancestors in the faith, and they find it easier to conform to secular norms of conduct than their parents did, especially when failure to conform might result in social disadvantage.

Over a lifetime, members of the society we live in seem able to profess adherence to various belief systems without significantly altering the way they live. Some have managed to compartmentalize their lives to such an extent that they do not allow their faith to manifest itself in any form of public behavior. The early Christian model was different. Those who demonstrated a desire to follow Christ were first shown a Christian way of life to imitate and offered help and encouragement in doing so. Doctrinal instruction came later. Quaker educator Parker J. Palmer, as I quoted earlier, describes the operative principle of such spiritual formation this way: "You don't think your way into a new kind of living; you live your way into a new kind of thinking."[3] Orthodox Christian blogger Clifton D. Healey asserts that contemporary efforts at evangelization in America tend to be centered on "a change of belief prior to a change of life." He writes,

> Modern attempts at witnessing focus on "relevance," and therapeutic solutions to life-critical scenarios (all oriented toward the improvement of one's own life) that will inexplicably occur simply by changing one's belief system. This is backward from the practice of ancient Christianity wherein converts were first inculcated in a way of life and then were [taught] the more systematic beliefs and doctrines that Christians held. Whereas today we seek salvation prior to conversion, ancient Christianity sought salvation through

---

of life in this world—not as a neat set of doctrines, an esoteric belief, or the promise of heaven. By practicing Jesus' teaching, followers of the way discovered that their lives were made better on a spiritual path. Indeed early Christianity was not called 'Christianity' at all. Rather, it was called 'the Way,' and its followers were called 'People of the Way.'"

2. See Kosmin and Keysar, *American*, 2. According to this most recent Trinity College American Religious Identification Survey, 76 percent of American adults identified as Christians in 2008, down from 86 percent in 1990.

3. Palmer, *Promise*, 60.

conversion. One did not register a "decision," later to be instructed in the faith. One first took on the way of life the church lived as an inextricable part of the process of conversion. *Ancient Christianity understood salvation not as a point in time but as a life-process extended through time and into eternity.*[4]

History has something to teach us. Living in a post-Christian Western civilization, there is much for contemporary Christians to learn from the way of life practiced by our forebearers in the three centuries before Christianity was embraced by Caesar. Second-century Christians' *way of life* is what made their *beliefs* attractive to those who lived among them, even though there were also in that society decent, moral, unselfish pagans to be found, whose lives were worthy of imitation. Christianity was attractive because in the world of late antiquity—at least by AD 200, perhaps sooner—Christians constituted the most widespread, coherent, charitable, merciful, moral, and deliberately inclusive religious community in many urban centers. Furthermore, the church was unique in welcoming converts from any stratum of that ancient, hierarchically ordered society. In this respect, Catholic Christians were markedly unlike gnostic Christians, because the Catholics were non-élitist; they opened their arms to everyone (this was the meaning of the adjective *katholikos*, "universal"). The Catholic Church embraced not only philosophical intellectuals, but men and women of both noble and common birth, slaves as well as free, literate and illiterate alike, as long as they acknowledged, confessed, and repented of their sins, turned to Jesus, were baptized, and committed themselves thereafter to follow Christ as Lord.

The Christian way of life did not require its adherents to engage in bizarre practices or separate themselves from non-Christian neighbors. It did link them to one another as members of a new kind of community, a sometimes ethnically and often socially diverse family of "brothers and sisters" who would be loyal to them and admonish them to persevere in their new way of life. Christian teaching did not impart to new followers of Jesus the idea that as Christians they were now better than everyone else. In fact, the church's teaching was exactly the opposite. Disciples were encouraged to treat others as more worthy than themselves and to show charity and mercy impartially to all. In his Letter to the Philippians, Paul exhorts them to imitate the humility of the Savior: "Do nothing from selfish ambition or conceit, but in humility regard others as better than yourselves. Let each

---

4. Healey, "Christianity," n.p. (italics added).

of you look not to your own interests, but to the interests of others. Let the same mind be in you that was in Christ Jesus" (Phil 2:3–5 NRSV).

In his book, *The Origins of Christian Morality*, Wayne Meeks shows that early Christian language of moral obligation differed little from that of the surrounding culture. Virtues the church expected its members to cultivate and vices they were expected to avoid were not unlike those named by the moralizing philosophers and rhetoricians of the time. Honesty, truthfulness, temperance, patience, loyalty, marital fidelity, and submissiveness to those in authority were to be practiced; theft, robbery, drunkenness, adultery, public scandal, and breach of trust were to be avoided. The only behavior expected in the Christian way of life that had never been regarded as a virtue in the Hellenistic world was *humility*.[5]

Christianity—along with Judaism—most clearly parted company with the rest of Greco-Roman society in its identification of an essential link between God and virtuous living. The church taught that Christian believers' transformed moral lives were the work of the Holy Spirit, whereas Hellenistic culture understood moral virtue as the product of a traditional philosophical education known as *paideia*—an education available only to a tiny, wealthy, sophisticated fraction of the population, not to shopkeepers, tradesmen, laborers, or slaves. In worshiping as God incarnate a man who had been subjected to the most dishonorable death imaginable in that society, Christian thinking turned the prevailing notions of honor and shame on their heads. And its assumption that the disciples of this crucified Galilean—who had now been raised from the dead and elevated to God's right hand in power—were the vanguard of a "new creation" (2 Cor 5:17) helped those same disciples live with a sense of hope and expectation utterly unknown to Hellenistic philosophy.

Unlike the traditional pagan cults, Christianity was an uncompromising faith, which ultimately led to its being regarded as a threat to Roman order. Followers of Jesus could serve only one God, not the pantheon of Greco-Roman divinities, and certainly not the "divinized" Caesars. This led to Christians being accused of atheism by their enemies. Followers of Jesus who refused to sacrifice to the genius of Caesar and Rome during the persecutions instigated under various emperors were officially condemned as disloyal because, as far as the state was concerned, only Caesar was Lord. For Christians, to say "Caesar is Lord"—even "with fingers crossed"—was

---

5. For a comparison of Christian and Hellenistic moral values, see Meeks, *Origins*, 15, 81–88.

apostasy. Of course, in times of state persecution, some Christians did apostatize to save their lives, and they were expelled from the communion of the church. Once persecution had ended, however, they sought to be restored to communion, confessing that they had only been cowards, not apostates. They hoped their publicly denied but secretly maintained convictions might somehow excuse their blasphemy.[6]

In this book, I have outlined how people in our time might restart their journey with Jesus, and I've done so out of the conviction that the spiritual formation of Christians must begin with commitment *to a person, Jesus, and to the way of life he taught*, not to a set of doctrines. That's why I wrote that the initial step in this process is the simple but momentous decision to undertake the remainder of one's life journey trusting Jesus as guide, recognizing that the mission of a disciple is to reproduce the life of the Master. Beginning with chapter 2, I described six events that logically proceed from that initial commitment to follow Christ, starting with searching and finding oneself in the great story of the Bible, coming to experience the love of God as Father, and then responding to God's love with worship, personal prayer, and finally the practice of self-offering love for others—which I associate with willingness to take up one's own cross and carry it with Jesus. I believe disciples who are willing to carry the cross will want to discern the higher purpose in life to which God is calling them. They are likely to say, in their own words, much the same thing Peter said when Jesus asked the Twelve if they were also going to abandon him, as others were doing who had found his teachings difficult: "Lord, to whom shall we go? You have the words of eternal life; and we have believed, and have come to know, that you are the Holy One of God" (John 6:69).

After those who have restarted their journey with Jesus have spent an extended period of time following the Lord and reflecting on that experience, meditating on Scripture, worshiping with a church, praying alone and with friends, and allowing the Spirit of God to work in their lives, they will have arrived at readiness to make a fresh and serious commitment to the church. The Episcopal Church, in whose ministry I serve, invites recommitted individuals (if they have already been baptized) to make a solemn

---

6. Apostates were automatically excommunicated from the Catholic Church, but they could make a public confession and ultimately be allowed to receive the Eucharist again, but only after years, sometimes decades, of humiliating public penance.

renewal of their Baptismal Covenant and receive the Bishop's laying on of hands. Other churches provide different ways of ritualizing such recommitments to Christ. In liturgical churches, those who make an act of recommitment are usually expected to make a public affirmation of the Apostles' Creed. Recommitted disciples will also likely be invited to give voice in a less formal way—out of their own experience—to what they personally believe about God, the saving work of Christ, and the empowering work of the Holy Spirit.

Anyone who has reached adulthood knows life is challenging, difficult, and rarely easy. Every one of us will face crises that will test our faith and defy our ability to persevere in a Christian way of life. All human beings, bar none, will encounter complex and painful situations. The following are just a few:

- We all will have to cope at some time with defeat, rejection, disappointment, loss, or grief. These challenging experiences still have power to make us question the love of God, even though they are a natural aspect of the human condition and we can expect to grapple with one or more of them.

- Skeptics will pose tough intellectual questions, and we will have no ready answer except to say, "I don't know." This is to be expected, but it may still leave us tormented by doubt.

- Moral dilemmas are sure to afflict us, and although we sincerely desire to follow Christ and do God's will, we're certain to face at least once—and perhaps more often—a forced choice in which the only available option is a decision for the lesser of two evils. When that happens, we may feel trapped, unsure of ourselves, and paralyzed by uncertainty.

- We will be tempted, often and in many different ways, and there will be times when we yield to those temptations. When we recognize our own weakness and moral failure, we may suffer the agony of guilt and fear that we have cut ourselves off from God.

- Finally, if we survive to old age, we must learn how to face the approach of death, and death might be preceded by a long illness and time of helplessness. If this is our experience, we may find ourselves feeling fragile and faithless, afraid to die and wondering whether the resurrection promise we have trusted is truly credible.

Putting It All Together: Christianity as a Way of Life

Taken together, these disturbing certainties (plus other scary uncertainties) have power to provoke us to anxiety and fear, which makes this the right point to recall what Jesus told his disciples on the night before he died: "In the world you have tribulation; but be of good cheer, I have overcome the world" (John 16:33). Twenty centuries of Christian history are rich with stories of holy men and women of every era who showed that walking in the steps of Jesus enables his disciples not only to endure and survive hardship and suffering, but to live in hope and joy, despite the many crises endemic to human existence. Through Jesus, his saints overcome the world. "Overcoming" is one way of describing life in the kingdom of God!

Human life is about change, letting go, putting off the old, and putting on the new. At first this might seem to be merely the observation of an older person whose life is mostly behind him, but in fact it describes the totality of human existence. It applies as well to a teenager graduating from high school as it does to a senior citizen coping with retirement. From the moment we come into the world, crying loudly because we've been expelled from the warmth and security of our mother's womb, until the day we leave this life behind and pass through the gate of death, human beings are required—either by our physical nature or our social circumstances—to engage in the repeated experience of letting go of things we once imagined as essential to our identity or our happiness and taking hold of new ways of living, learning, and serving that are appropriate to the current stage of our life's journey. To borrow the language of Paul, until we "take off" the outworn or outgrown attributes of our former life, we cannot "put on" the new, "created after the likeness of God in true righteousness and holiness" (Eph 4:22–24). We can't have a new life if we won't let go of the old one. This thought is conveyed by Jesus' paradoxical saying, "those who want to save their life will lose it, and those who lose their life for my sake will save it" (Luke 9:24 NRSV). And, of course, as a part of this journey upward with Jesus, we must abandon the grudges, resentments, and bad memories that threaten to trap us in the past. We most successfully survive the tailspins of heartache and loss by moving on with our lives and leaving our grievances behind us.[7]

---

7. See Au, *Enduring*, 21–38. Au presents a thoughtful presentation of the role of "letting go" in the disciple's way of life.

Finding the Way

The Christian way of life grows out of a chosen perspective of radical trust in the loving providence of our *Abba*. The decision to believe in God and trust ourselves to him as we walk in the footsteps of Jesus is not a decision that can ever be made once for all time. Instead, it's a decision each person who perseveres on the journey must make daily, because the claims and temptations of the world are ever present, inviting us to choose different paths. Those who would keep faith with Jesus are compelled to abandon themselves daily to the providence of God and put their lives in God's hands. Charles de Foucauld, whose books and sacrificial life among the Tuareg people of the Sahara inspired the Roman Catholic lay and religious communities known as Jesus Caritas and the Little Brothers and Little Sisters of Jesus, composed this "Prayer of Abandonment to God." Its expression of absolute trust in God makes it worth memorizing.

> Father,
> I abandon myself into your hands;
> do with me what you will.
> Whatever you may do, I thank you;
> I am ready for all, I accept all.
> Let only your will be done in me,
> and in all your creatures.
> I wish no more than this, O Lord.
> Into your hands I commend my soul;
> I offer it to you with all the love of my heart,
> for I love you, Lord,
> and so need to give myself,
> to surrender myself into your hands,
> without reserve,
> and with boundless confidence,
> for you are my Father.[8]

We who are hungry for God will not find our hunger satisfied simply by a system of doctrine, no matter how philosophically profound, but by a pattern for living in the world that we can learn to follow. A way of life that does not equip us to pass through the inevitable pains and hardships of life without being crippled by them has little to recommend it. A way of life that enables us not only to survive the traumas of human existence, but to experience incomprehensible peace and the joy of God's presence in spite of them, is eminently desirable. This is the way of life Christians proclaim to the world: the way of Christ, the journey with Jesus. It is a way that has

---

8. Foucauld, "Prayer of Abandonment," as quoted by Carretto, *Summoned*, 19.

been followed by countless saints for two thousand years. It is the way that was followed by Paul, who wrote this message to his friends from a Roman prison:

> Rejoice in the Lord always; again I will say, Rejoice. Let your gentleness be known to everyone. The Lord is near. Do not worry about anything, but in everything by prayer and supplication with thanksgiving let your requests be made known to God. And the peace of God, which surpasses all understanding, will guard your hearts and your minds in Christ Jesus. . . . I have learned to be content with whatever I have. I know what it is to have little, and I know what it is to have plenty. In any and all circumstances I have learned the secret of being well-fed and of going hungry, of having plenty and of being in need. I can do all things through him who strengthens me (Phil 4:4–7, 11b–13 NRSV).

Finding the Way

༄ ༄ ༄

For Your Reflection

*After reading chapter 9,
"Putting It All Together:Christianity as a Way of Life"*

- In the past, did you think about Christianity more as a "belief system" or as a "way of life"? Why?

- Think about your discretionary spending in the past year. To what extent were your personal decisions about spending for things other than food, housing, and other necessities based on what you believe? To what extent were they based simply on your appetites and feelings? Would you say that your beliefs (and the values they express) rather than your appetites guide your discretionary spending most of the time? Half the time? Rarely?

- Spend some time thinking about this passage from the Letter of James. In reflecting on this passage, think of the word *faith* here as applying to beliefs and the word *works* as applying to behavior (actions).

  > What good is it, my brothers and sisters, if you say you have faith but do not have works? Can faith save you? If a brother or sister is naked and lacks daily food, and one of you says to them, "Go in peace; keep warm and eat your fill," and yet you do not supply their bodily needs, what is the good of that? So faith by itself, if it has no works, is dead. But someone will say, "You have faith and I have works." Show me your faith apart from your works, and I by my works will show you my faith. You believe that God is one; you do well. Even the demons believe—and shudder. Do you want to be shown, you senseless person, that faith apart from works is barren? Was not our ancestor Abraham justified by works when he offered his son Isaac on the altar? You see that faith was active along with his works, and faith was brought to completion by the works. Thus the Scripture was fulfilled that says, "Abraham believed God, and it was reckoned to him as righteousness," and he was called the friend of God (James 2:14–23 NRSV).

- Describe your understanding of what Parker J. Palmer meant when he wrote, "You don't think your way into a new kind of living; you live your way into a new kind of thinking."

Putting It All Together: Christianity as a Way of Life

- What are some behaviors you now feel ready to undertake that may transform your way of thinking?
- Put these behaviors into the form of a personal Rule of Life.[9]

---

9. See http://ruleoflife.com, a website devoted to this subject, entitled *Crafting a Rule of Life: An Invitation to the Well-Ordered Way*. See also http://renovare.org. Renovaré is an organization that provides spiritual formation resources, particularly in the area of spiritual disciplines. The books by Richard Foster and Dallas Willard listed in appendix B also provide guidance and encouragement for disciples who want to develop a personal Rule of Life.

Epilogue: Jesus Is Looking for Disciples, Not Admirers

THIS BOOK IS FOR people who want to make the journey of life with Jesus. The middle of Luke's gospel is a narrative of Jesus' own journey on the long, winding road up from Galilee to Jerusalem, a journey he was sure would end with his death. Luke describes Jesus' attitude in these words: "As the days drew near for him to be taken up, he *set his face to go to Jerusalem*" (9:51, italics added). Jesus had a destination, and he "set his face" to reach it. That's a very telling expression!

A compliment often given Olympic athletes, serious musicians, missionaries, and others deeply committed to a particular goal in life is to describe them as *focused*—people whose eyes are fixed on a destination, no matter how distant, that they intend to reach, regardless of what stands in the way. These are tough-minded people whose "faces are set." Focus, commitment, tenacity—by whatever name we call it, it's a virtue we admire. When Luke said Jesus "set his face to go to Jerusalem," he meant Jesus was resolved to do God's will, regardless what that obedience would cost him.

He had already told his closest friends he was on his way to certain death. He had enemies; and he had no illusions about what was waiting for him in the capital city. Jesus knew that in Jerusalem there would be a battle between the incarnate love of God and the power of this world's darkness. By this point in his ministry he was sure he would have to die in order for the loving intention of God to triumph over evil. But he also had faith in his Father and trusted that if he gave himself up to death, God would raise him up.

The middle of the Third Gospel is a narrative of Jesus' journey from Galilee up to Jerusalem and the cross. He's portrayed as always on the way, walking the road, passing through countryside, villages, and towns. As he keeps moving, we see that neither his disciples nor the people to whom he speaks entirely comprehend what's in store for him. They know he's going to Jerusalem, but most of them believe the journey to the capital should be a kind of triumphant parade. Jesus is clearly wise, holy, brave, charismatic, and amazing. He looks like God's "Man of the Moment." Therefore, it seems obvious and proper that he should be acclaimed as the Lord's Anointed by the leaders of the nation when he arrives on their doorstep.

Because of this, Jesus attracts a crowd of tagalongs as he moves closer to the Holy City. Most of them are admirers, not followers—people we'd call "fans" today, rather than disciples. They go with him because they're eager to see the victory of their hero. They want to be eyewitnesses to the anticipated miracles that are sure to put awe in the hearts of the chief priests and elders. No doubt, they compose most of the "multitude" of followers who Luke tells us accompany Jesus, praising God "joyfully with a loud voice for all the deeds of power that they had seen, saying, *'Blessed is the king who comes in the name of the Lord!'*" as he rides down the Mount of Olives into the city on a borrowed donkey on Sunday morning (Luke 19:37–38 NRSV, italics added).

But some of the people who join Jesus on the way to Jerusalem are much more than members of his fan club. They are the ones who paid the most attention when earlier he gave voice to premonitions of tragedy, and now they're concerned about what could happen when he gets to the city. But this worry does not dissuade them from following him, because they are deeply serious about their bond with Jesus. They want to share his life—and even his death, if need be. (Or so they think *now*, though we know that when his enemies strike on Thursday night they—like the Twelve—will abandon him to his fate.)

Jesus was never interested in merely casual or opportunistic followers. He had no time for fair-weather friends—the fans who wanted to follow him simply to be amazed by miracles or to applaud impressive sermons. And Jesus made no glib, shallow promises to the crowd in order to curry favor. His manner was totally opposite from that of many politicians and so-called spiritual leaders of our time. He refused to exploit his popularity for any kind of gain, and he never soft-peddled the cost of discipleship. To a man who claimed he was ready to follow Jesus anywhere, he said, "Are you sure? Even if you have to sleep by the roadside? Even if nobody in town will rent you a room because you're with me? Keep in mind that the Son of Man, on this very journey, has not even had a place to lay his head." The level of devotion Jesus asked for was total. To a man who said he'd follow

Epilogue: Jesus Is Looking for Disciples, Not Admirers

Jesus as soon as he'd buried his father, Jesus said, "Come with me and leave the dead to bury their own dead." To another who only wanted permission to run back home and kiss his parents goodbye before joining the band of disciples, Jesus said, "Nobody who puts his hand to the plow and looks back is fit for the kingdom of heaven."[1] We can't miss Jesus' message here.

In a slim volume called *Practice in Christianity*, which Søren Kierkegaard regarded as his "most perfect and truest book,"[2] the famous Danish theologian wrote,

> It is well known that Christ consistently used the expression "follower." He never asks for admirers, worshippers, or adherents. No, he calls disciples. It is not adherents of a teaching but followers of a life Christ is looking for.
>
> Christ understood that being a "disciple" was in innermost and deepest harmony with what he said about himself. Christ claimed to be the way and the truth and the life (Jn. 14:6). For this reason, he could never be satisfied with adherents who accepted his teaching – especially with those who in their lives ignored it or let things take their usual course. *His whole life on earth, from beginning to end, was destined solely to have followers and to make admirers impossible* [italics added].
>
> Christ came into the world with the purpose of saving, not instructing it. At the same time – as is implied in his saving work – he came to be *the pattern* [italics in original], to leave footprints for the person who would join him, who would become a follower.... What then, is the difference between an admirer and a follower? A follower *is* or strives *to be* what he admires [italics in original]. An admirer, however, keeps himself personally detached. He fails to see that what is admired involves a claim upon him, and thus he fails to be or strive to be what he admires.[3]

If we really want to be Jesus' disciples and not just members of his fan club, we must know that he expects us to set our faces the way he set his own and keep walking with him in the way of the cross. The truth is, Jesus has always attracted more admirers than disciples, more fans than followers. Admirers

---

1. See Luke 9:57–62.
2. Willimon, "Impractical Christianity," 224.
3. Kierkegaard, "Followers," 85–86, as excerpted by Moore from *Practice in Christianity*.

Finding the Way

of Jesus are everywhere, and they have always said nice things about him, such as, "He was a wise man, a good man, the best man who ever lived." Or, "He was noble, kind, compassionate, self-sacrificing, and full of love for everybody." (After all, what's not to admire about Jesus?) But *admirers* are not *disciples*. Here is the difference:

- Admirers are spectators. They want to watch, listen, and applaud (and sometimes feel free to boo). Disciples want to be participants, get involved.
- Admirers want to appreciate Jesus. Disciples want to imitate Jesus.
- Admirers lose interest when they're no longer being entertained or stimulated, or when there's no immediate payoff. Disciples want to go where Jesus is going, even if the trail leading there is steep and icy.
- Admirers feel no responsibility to Jesus. They regard themselves as independent and autonomous. Disciples have a sense of responsibility; they understand it's their duty to reproduce the life of the Master.

Listen to Kierkegaard again:

> The admirer never makes any true sacrifices. He always plays it safe. Though in words, phrases, songs, he is inexhaustible about how highly he prizes Christ, he renounces nothing, gives up nothing, will not reconstruct his life, will not be what he admires, and will not let his life express what it is he supposedly admires. Not so for the follower. No, no. The follower aspires with all his strength, with all his will to be what he admires. And then, remarkably enough, even though he is living amongst a "Christian people," the same danger results for him as was once the case when it was dangerous to openly confess Christ. And because of the follower's life, it will become evident who the admirers are, for the admirers will become agitated with him.[4]

The spiritual marketplace is an inescapable aspect of our consumer-oriented age, an expression of our insistence on free choice, our need to celebrate private preference. Having liberty to choose is a good thing, not a bad thing. *But what shall we choose? And for what reasons shall we choose it?* One may find preachers and spiritual entrepreneurs of many kinds in America today: Christian, pseudo-Christian, and non-Christian, teachers of eastern religions, advocates of western secularism, and even people touting the lunacy of cults. It's a carnival of souls out there.

4. Kierkegaard, "Practice," 87.

Epilogue: Jesus Is Looking for Disciples, Not Admirers

We have friends who are shopping and hopping from one religion or cult or church to another and back again, looking for a teacher who will provide the custom-tailored spiritual experience they're after, and who will promise them absolute certainty that they now are, *finally*, on The One True Path to serenity or prosperity or transcendence. Last time we talked, our friends were Lutherans (or Episcopalians or Methodists), but now they're serious about Tantric Buddhism. Next year maybe they'll be studying Scientology. After that, who knows? Possibly Wicca.

But here is one thing all of us know is true: the greatest peace, the most "centered" place in human life, is found when we commit to *one* Master, *one* Guide, *one* Lord—and stick with Him. We will never find peace if we're always looking for someone or something new: another new guru, another new hero, or another new way of life.

For me, and for many of you who have been reading this book, Jesus is the *One*. We know he's not looking for another admirer. He has plenty of them, always has and always will. But Jesus is looking for another true follower, another disciple whose mission is to reproduce the life of the Master. Jesus is looking for

 . . . somebody who's ready to commit,

 . . . somebody who's able to be focused,

 . . . somebody who can "set his face" or "set her face" and keep walking the upward trail in Jesus' footsteps, no matter how slippery the going gets.

Is that "somebody" *you*?[5]

---

5. This epilogue was previously published in a different form in McNab, *Let Your Light Shine*, 181–186.

Appendix A

Bibles and Bible Reading

Bibles

FOR PEOPLE WHO WANT to start reading the Bible regularly, it's important to choose a version of the Bible that you will feel is easy and pleasant to read—and this means both physically comfortable (in terms of the bulk of the book and the size of the print) as well as understandable. There are many versions to choose from, and nearly all of them can be found in a wide variety of bindings and print sizes.

It might be interesting to know that the books of the New Testament were originally written not merely in Greek, but in what we must call "common" Greek—the language of everyday life—rather than the formal Attic Greek of philosophers, poets, and lawyers. New Testament Greek was the language of the streets, full of idiomatic expressions and not always grammatically correct. It was lively and simple. It's the kind of language most of us use when we're talking to our friends. On the other hand, the Hebrew Scriptures are the definitive texts of "classical" Hebrew. This means that when we're reading an English translation of the Bible, we might reasonably expect the books of the Old Testament to seem more formal and traditional in style, while the books of the New Testament are more relaxed or even colloquial.

For the English language, the King James Version of the Bible might be said to define "classical" English style—along with the works of Shakespeare and the 1662 Book of Common Prayer. Both the Old Testament and New Testament may seem archaic and formal to modern Americans when we hear them read from the KJV. More modern versions might work better if you are looking for a Bible for personal reading. One way to find a Bible

Appendix A

that will suit you is to talk to Christian friends and ask them what versions they like best. Or go to a good bookstore and thumb through the various Bibles that are for sale. Compare one with another in terms of their readability. Compare the same verse in several different versions.

There are many different English translations of the Scriptures, plus a few useful paraphrases. A *translation* makes an effort to render the original Hebrew or Greek into understandable English. There are a variety of translation philosophies. Some versions of the Bible attempt to provide a *literal* translation, insofar as that is possible. They attempt to provide an English word for every Greek or Hebrew word, and, when that is not possible, to give as literal a rendering as possible, regardless of the sense of the resulting English. Other versions attempt to provide an *interpretive* translation. These interpretive versions try to "make sense" of the ancient Hebrew or Greek words and expressions in contemporary English.

The various available English versions range on a spectrum from the very literal to the very interpretative. For example, The New American Standard Bible (NASB) is a very literal translation, as is the much more recent and quite popular English Standard Version (ESV), while the Today's English Version (TEV), also called the Good News Bible, and the Contemporary English Version (CEV) are very interpretive versions in mostly American English, produced by the American Bible Society. The New English Bible (NEB) is a moderately interpretive version in British English. The very popular New International Version (NIV) is a moderately interpretive version, which can be purchased in either American or British English editions. The New American Bible, Revised Edition (NABRE) is an official Roman Catholic version in contemporary English. The first major update to the New American Bible text in 20 years was approved for publication in 2011. Although it is an officially authorized Roman Catholic translation of the Bible, there is nothing in the text that should prove problematic to Protestants, although the notes and study aids are Roman Catholic in their orientation.

The New Revised Standard Version (NRSV) is a middle-of-the-road translation, neither woodenly literal nor too interpretive. Its text is the result of an effort to create a careful, but gender-neutral, "non-sexist" translation. It preserves the masculine personal pronouns in reference to God, but generally rephrases other personal references to make them plural (when that would not change the sense of the original), using the inclusive pronoun "they" in place of the masculine pronoun "he" found in the original text.

Appendix A

People who want to read a familiar-sounding, modern English version, but want to catch the original pronouns and have a slightly more literal text than the NRSV might prefer the older Revised Standard Version (RSV), which the NRSV was originally meant to supersede.

If you would like a very contemporary-sounding, informal, even colloquial version of the Scriptures, you might examine *The Living Bible*, *The Message: The Bible in Contemporary Language* (by Eugene H. Peterson), and *The New Testament in Modern English* (by J. B. Phillips). These are *paraphrases*, not translations, strictly speaking. They are highly interpretive, not literal. All three are quite readable, but I recommend that you also keep one of the more literal translations on hand to compare what the original "really" says with what you find in the paraphrase. Of the three paraphrases, the one I like best is *The Message*. It makes use of appropriate contemporary English colloquial expressions in places where the Hebrew or Greek originals made use of colloquial expressions that were apt for their own time.

This appendix is meant to guide those who are reading the Bible as an act of prayer. For those who want to engage in biblical study, it is best to have a variety of different translations on hand, as well as at least one good paraphrase, in order to compare them with one another.

Bible Reading

There are a variety of reasons a person might have for reading the Bible, not all of which have anything to do with seeking to build a relationship with God. My hope is that you who read *Finding the Way* will want to read the Bible for spiritual reasons: because you believe God "speaks" to men and women of every age and culture through its words, and you want to hear God for yourselves. You want to ponder the wisdom of God. You want to know the will of God. You want to draw close to God. You want to meditate on the truth found in Scripture and let that meditation deepen your faith and your love for God. You want to "find yourselves in the Sacred Story," as I said in chapter 2, and thus come to a deeper knowledge of your own true selves.

If you're seeking to deepen your relationship with God, there is no single best program for reading the Bible. Individuals must determine what works best for them. The important thing is to create sacred space in your life every day for prayer and the reading of Scripture. The two go hand in hand. In fact, I think reading the Bible is a form of prayer if you read the

Appendix A

Bible in order to turn yourself to God. Michael Casey, an Australian Cistercian writer on spirituality, has published a book entitled *Sacred Reading*, which is a guide to the kind of slow, meditative reading of Scripture that I recommend.

For this kind of prayerful approach to Scripture, I suggest that you read a portion of Scripture slowly and reflectively, not trying to analyze it, but simply hear it with the ear of the heart and allow it to penetrate your soul. Since your heart's desire is to follow Jesus on the journey of life, it's best to begin with meditating on the gospels, especially if you're just beginning to be a daily Bible reader. Start with Mark, which was probably the first gospel written, then move on to Matthew. After reading Matthew, I recommend you skip to John, and after reading John, then read Luke, followed by the book of Acts. Luke wrote both the gospel called by his name and the book of Acts. Acts is really the sequel to Luke, and it's good to read them in tandem.

When you start out with a new book, give yourself time to read it through in a single sitting. None of the books of the New Testament are so long that you won't be able to do that, but it might be best to do this on a day when you are not pressed for time. After reading Mark straight through, the next day go back to the beginning of Mark and read until something particularly touches you. Go no further, but rather read that portion again. Spend some time reflecting on the passage, allowing it to speak to you, and then pray. The following day, in your time for Scripture and prayer, resume at the point where you stopped reading the previous day. Do the same thing: read until something particularly touches you, then stop and reread that portion, spend time in reflection on it, and then pray. Make this your pattern until you have completed Mark. Then read Matthew through in one sitting, and the next day start with the first chapter of Matthew and read it just as you read Mark. Then move to John, and to Luke/Acts, doing the same thing with each book. After reading the four gospels and the book of Acts, proceed to Paul's Epistle to the Romans and go on through the New Testament.

Before starting to read the Old Testament, it would probably be helpful to read a general introduction to the Bible, such as *Introducing the Bible* by William Barclay. This is an old book, but it's perfect for someone just beginning to read the Bible regularly. If you are a beginner, rather than reading through the entire Old Testament in your sacred reading time, I suggest confining yourself to these books (reading them in the same way I

Appendix A

described for reading the New Testament): Genesis, Exodus, Deuteronomy, 1 and 2 Samuel, 1 and 2 Kings, Isaiah, Jeremiah, Hosea, Joel, Amos, and Micah.

Although there are no perfect plans for reading the Bible, there are a great many plans available. If you do a web search on the term "Bible reading plans," you will find literally millions of choices. The publishers of the new English Standard Version (ESV) have ten different reading plans posted on their website (www.esv.org/resources/reading-plans-devotions/), each of which may be downloaded in your choice of five different formats, including one for mobile phones.

There are also printed (and e-book) editions of the Bible arranged for daily reading. Here are two examples: (1) *The Message//REMIX 2.0 Pause: A Daily Reading Bible*. This special edition of *The Message* Bible paraphrase is organized for daily readings that will take the reader through the entire Bible in one year, two years, or four years. Its book-at-a-time reading plan immerses one in an Old Testament and a New Testament passage daily, with a programmed time for reflection each seventh day. (2) *Today's Light Bible* (NIV). This edition of the NIV is set up to take a reader through the Bible in two years. It starts with "Week 1, Monday," with no dates. It also provides no Sunday readings. Each reading starts with a brief introduction to the reading, called "Get the Big Picture." Each is followed by a brief devotion called "Sharpen the Focus." The readings are short enough to allow a novice Bible reader to complete them every day.

Those who wish to live a Christian way of life *need* the Bible. It opens us to the personal history of Jesus himself and his experience of the Father and the Spirit. It shows us how those who knew him best responded to their experience of his life, his words, his deeds, and his death and resurrection. Without pondering the Scriptures we can never truly be his disciples, never truly have "the mind of Christ."

Appendix B

Recommended Books

THERE ARE ABUNDANT PUBLISHED resources available to support and encourage people restarting their journey with Jesus. In this appendix, I list only books that I have read and think are worth recommending.

Allen, Diogenes. *Quest: The Search for Meaning through Christ*. New York: Church, 2000.

———. *Theology for a Troubled Believer: An Introduction to the Christian Faith*. Louisville: Westminster John Knox, 2010.

Au, Wilkie. *The Enduring Heart: Spirituality for the Long Haul*. New York: Paulist, 2000.

Barclay, William. *Introducing the Bible*. Revised by John Rogerson. Nashville: Abingdon, 1997.

Bass, Diana Butler. *Christianity after Religion: The End of Church and the Birth of a New Spiritual Awakening*. New York: HarperOne, 2012.

Bell, Rob. *Love Wins: A Book about Heaven, Hell, and the Fate of Everyone Who Ever Lived*. New York: HarperOne, 2011.

Boulding, Maria. *Prayer: Our Journey Home*. Ann Arbor, MI: Servant, 1980.

Brother Lawrence. *The Practice of the Presence of God*. New Kensington, PA: Whitaker, 1982.

Buechner, Frederick. *Wishful Thinking: A Theological ABC*. New York: Harper & Row, 1973.

Carretto, Carlo. *Summoned by Love*. Translate by Alan Neame. Maryknoll, NY: Orbis, 1978.

Casey, Michael. *Fully Human, Fully Divine: An Interactive Christology*. Liguori, MO: Liguori/Triumph, 2004.

Appendix B

———. *Sacred Reading: The Ancient Art of Lectio Divina*. Liguori, MO: Liguori/Triumph, 1996.

———. *Toward God: The Ancient Wisdom of Western Prayer*. Liguori, MO: Liguori/Triumph, 1996. Revised edition of *Towards God*, 1989.

Caussade, Jean-Pierre de. *Abandonment to Divine Providence*. Translated by John Beevers. Garden City: Doubleday Image, 1975.

Évely, Louis. *Our Prayer*. Translated by Paul Burns. New York: Herder and Herder, 1970.

———. *We Are All Brothers: Gospel Meditations on Brotherly Love*. Translated by Mary Agnes. Garden City: Doubleday Image, 1975.

Foster, Richard J. *Celebration of Discipline: The Path to Spiritual Growth*. San Francisco: Harper & Row, 1978.

Frey, William C. *The Dance of Hope: Finding Ourselves in the Rhythm of God's Great Story*. Colorado Springs: WaterBrook, 2003.

Hall, Thelma. *Too Deep for Words: Rediscovering Lectio Divina*. New York: Paulist, 1988.

Hauerwas, Stanley, and William H. Willimon. *Resident Aliens: Life in the Christian Colony*. Nashville: Abingdon, 1989.

Jones, Alan W. *Journey into Christ*. New York: Seabury, 1977.

Lewis, C. S. *The Four Loves*. New York: Harcourt Brace Jovanovich, 1991. Reprint. Originally published by Harcourt, Brace, 1960.

———. *God in the Dock: Essays on Theology and Ethics*. Grand Rapids: Eerdmans, 1970.

———. *Mere Christianity*. Revised edition. New York: HarperOne, 2001.

Lyons, Gabe. *The Next Christians: The Good News about the End of Christian America*. New York: Doubleday, 2010.

McLaren, Brian. *A Generous Orthodoxy*. Grand Rapids: Zondervan, 2004.

Merton, Thomas. *No Man is an Island*. New York: Harcourt, Brace, 1955.

———. *Thoughts in Solitude*. New York: Farrar, Straus and Giroux, 1958.

Nouwen, Henri J. M. *Reaching Out: The Three Movements of the Spiritual Life*. Garden City, NY: Doubleday, 1975.

O'Driscoll, Herbert. *A Doorway in Time*. San Francisco: Harper & Row, 1985.

Powell, Mark Allan. *Loving Jesus*. Minneapolis: Fortress, 2004.

Rohr, Richard. *Falling Upward: A Spirituality for the Two Halves of Life*. San Francisco: Jossey-Bass, 2011.

———. *Hope Against Darkness: The Transforming Vision of St. Francis in an Age of Anxiety*. Cincinnati: St. Anthony Messenger, 2001.

———. *Things Hidden: Scripture as Spirituality.* Cincinnati: St. Anthony Messenger, 2008.

Rolheiser, Ronald. *Against an Infinite Horizon: The Finger of God in our Everyday Lives.* Revised edition. New York: Crossroad, 2001.

———. *The Holy Longing: The Search for Christian Spirituality.* New York: Doubleday, 1999.

———. *The Shattered Lantern: Rediscovering a Felt Presence of God.* New York: Crossroad, 2004.

Simons, Joseph and Jeanne Reidy. *The Risk of Loving.* New York: Seabury, 1973.

Willard, Dallas. *The Spirit of the Disciplines: Understanding How God Changes Lives.* San Francisco: HarperSanFrancisco, 1988.

Willimon, William H. *Who Will Be Saved?* Nashville: Abingdon, 2008.

Wright, N. T. *Scripture and the Authority of God.* London: SPCK, 2005.

———. *Simply Christian: Why Christianity Makes Sense.* San Fransisco: HarperSanFrancisco, 2006.

Bibliography

Allen, Diogenes. *Theology for a Troubled Believer: An Introduction to the Christian Faith.* Louisville: Westminster John Knox, 2010.
Armstrong, Karen. *The Case for God.* New York: Anchor, 2009.
Au, Wilkie. *The Enduring Heart: Spirituality for the Long Haul.* New York: Paulist, 2000,
Augustine. *Confessions.* Translated by Garry Wills. New York: Penguin, 2006.
Barker, Margaret. "Isaiah." In *Eerdmans Commentary on the Bible*, edited by James D. G. Dunn and John W. Rogerson, 489–542. Grand Rapids: Eerdmans, 2003.
Bass, Diana Butler. *Christianity after Religion: The End of Church and the Birth of a New Spiritual Awakening.* New York: HarperOne, 2012.
Beck, Richard. "Letters from Cell 92: Part 6, 'The Man for Others.'" *Experimental Theology*, December 19, 2010. Online: http://experimentaltheology.blogspot.com/2010/12/letters-from-cell-92-part-6-man-for.html.
Bell, Rob. *Love Wins: A Book about Heaven, Hell, and the Fate of Every Person Who Ever Lived.* New York: HarperOne, 2011.
Blow, Charles. "Spirit Quest." *New York Times*, February 20, 2010.
The Book of Common Prayer. New York: Church Publishing, 1986.
Boulding, Maria. *Prayer: Our Journey Home.* Ann Arbor, MI: Servant, 1980.
Brother Lawrence. *The Practice of the Presence of God.* New Kensington, PA: Whitaker, 1982.
Brown, Raymond E. *The Gospel According to John 1–12.* The Anchor Bible 29. Garden City, NY: Doubleday, 1966.
Buechner, Frederick. *Wishful Thinking: A Theological ABC.* New York: Harper & Row, 1973.
Campolo, Tony. "If I Should Wake Before I Die." *Thirty Good Minutes* 3627. Transcribed from tape and edited for clarity. First broadcast April 25, 1993. Online: http://www.csec.org/index.php/archives/23-member-archives/737-tony-campolo-program-3627.
Carretto, Carlo. *Summoned by Love.* Translated by Alan Neame. Maryknoll, NY: Orbis, 1978.
Casey, Michael. *Fully Human, Fully Divine: An Interactive Christology.* Liguori, MO: Liguori/Triumph, 2004.
―――. *Sacred Reading: The Ancient Art of Lectio Divina.* Liguori, MO: Liguori/Triumph, 1996.
―――. *Toward God: The Ancient Wisdom of Western Prayer.* Liguori, MO: Liguori/Triumph, 1996. Revised edition of *Towards God*, 1989.
Caussade, Jean-Pierre de. *Abandonment to Divine Providence.* Translated by John Beevers. Garden City, NY: Image, 1975.

Bibliography

Duff, Nancy. "Reformed Theology and Medical Ethics: Death, Vocation, and the Suspension of Life Support." In *Toward the Future of Reformed Theology: Tasks, Topics, Tradition*, edited by David Willis and Michael Welker, 302–18. Grand Rapids: Eerdmans, 1999.

Encyclopaedia Britannica. "Saint Francis of Assisi." Online: http://www.britannica.com/EBchecked/topic/216793/Saint-Francis-of-Assisi.

Évely, Louis. *We Are All Brothers: Gospel Meditations on Brotherly Love.* Translated by Mary Agnes. Garden City, NY: Image, 1975.

Feynman, Richard. "The Pleasure of Finding Things Out: Doubt and Uncertainty." BBC *Horizon* video 0:53. Interview from 1981. Online: http://www.bbc.co.uk/sn/tvradio/programmes/horizon/broadband/archive/feynman/.

Funk, Cary, and Greg Smith. "'Nones' on the Rise: One-in-Five Adults Have No Religious Affiliation." Pew Research Center's Forum on Religion & Public Life, October, 2012. Online: http://www.pewforum.org/uploadedFiles/Topics/Religious_Affiliation/Unaffiliated/NonesontheRise-full.pdf.

Gilgoff, Dan. "Many Americans Are Saying Goodbye to Religion, but Not Faith." *U.S. News & World Report.* May 6, 2009. Online: http://www.usnews.com/news/religion/articles/2009/05/06/many-americans-are-saying-goodbye-to-religion-but-not-faith.

Gregg, Carol M. "Discover 'Vocation': An Essay on the Concept of Vocation." *Journal of College and Character* 6, no. 1 (2005):1–7.

Hanson, R. P. C. *The Attractiveness of God: Essays in Christian Doctrine.* Richmond, VA: John Knox, 1974.

Hauerwas, Stanley, and William H. Willimon. *Resident Aliens: Life in the Christian Colony.* Nashville: Abingdon, 1989.

Hayes, Richard B. *The Moral Vision of the New Testament: Community, Cross, New Creation: A Contemporary Introduction to New Testament Ethics.* San Francisco: HarperSanFrancisco, 1996.

Healy, Clifton D. "Christianity as *Philosophia* and Evangelization." *This Is Life!: Revolutions around the Cruciform Axis* (blog). July 1, 2005. Online: http://benedictseraphim.wordpress.com/2005/07/01/christianity-as-philosophia-and-evangelization/.

Hunter, James Davison. *To Change the World: The Irony, Tragedy, and Possibility of Christianity in the Late Modern World.* New York: Oxford University Press, 2010.

Jones, Alan W. *Journey into Christ.* New York: Seabury, 1977.

Julian. *The Works of the Emperor Julian.* Vol. 3. Translated by Wilmer C. Wright. Loeb Classical Library 157. Cambridge, MA: Harvard University Press, 1913.

Julian of Norwich. *Revelations of Divine Love.* Grand Rapids, MI: *Christian Classics Ethereal Library*, 2005. First published London: Methuen, 1901. Online as e-book: http://www.ccel.org/ccel/julian/revelations.pdf.

Kidder, Tracy. *Mountains Beyond Mountains: The Quest of Dr. Paul Farmer, a Man Who Would Cure the World.* New York: Random House, 2003.

Kierkegaard, Søren. "Followers Not Admirers." In *Provocations: Spiritual Writings of Søren Kierkegaard*, 85–88. Compiled and edited by Charles E. Moore. Rifton. NY: Plough, 2011. Online as e-book: http://cdn.plough.com/~/media/Files/Plough/ebooks/pdfs/p/provocationsEN.pdf.

Kosmin, Barry A., and Ariela Keysar. *American Religious Identification Survey (ARIS 2008) Summary Report.* Hartford, CT: Trinity College Institute for the Study of Secularism in Society & Culture, 2009.

Bibliography

Leech, Kenneth. *Experiencing God: Theology as Spirituality*. New York: Harper & Row, 1985.

———. *True Prayer: An Invitation to Christian Spirituality*. San Francisco: Harper & Row, 1980.

Lewis, C. S. *The Four Loves*. New York: Harcourt Brace Jovanovich, 1991.

Llewelyn, Robert. "Prayer and Contemplation." In *Praying Home: The Contemplative Journey*, 1–59. Cambridge, MA: Cowley, 1987.

Lose, David. "Do Christian Denominations Have a Future?" *Huffington Post*. June 22, 2012. Online: http://www.huffingtonpost.com/david-lose/christian-denominations-over_b_1616233.html.

McNab, Bruce. *Let Your Light Shine*. Bloomington, IN: Xlibris, 2010.

Meeks, Wayne A. *The Origins of Christian Morality*. New Haven, CT: Yale University Press, 1993.

Merton, Thomas. *Opening the Bible*. Collegeville, MN: Liturgical, 1986.

———. *The Seven Storey Mountain*. New York: Harcourt, Brace, 1948.

———. *Thoughts in Solitude*. New York: Farrar, Straus and Giroux, 1999.

Miller, Joel J. "God Made Us to Love Us." *Patheos*. February 4, 2011. Online: http://www.patheos.com/blogs/joeljmiller/2011/02/god-made-us-to-love-us-so-we-can-love-too/.

New World Encyclopedia. "Metanarrative." Online: http://www.newworldencyclopedia.org/entry/metanarrative.

Newport, Frank. "More than 9 in 10 Americans Continue to Believe in God: Professed Belief Is Lower Among Younger Americans, Easterners, and Liberals." *Gallup*. June 3, 2011. Online: http://www.gallup.com/poll/147887/americans-continue-believe-god.aspx.

Nouwen, Henri J. M. *Reaching Out: The Three Movements of the Spiritual Life*. Garden City, NY: Doubleday, 1975.

O'Driscoll, Herbert. *A Doorway in Time*. San Francisco: Harper & Row, 1985.

Palmer, Parker J. *Let Your Life Speak: Listening for the Voice of Vocation*. San Francisco: Jossey-Bass, 2000.

———. *The Promise of Paradox: A Celebration of Contradictions in the Christian Life*. Notre Dame, IN: Ave Maria, 1980.

Piatt, Christian. "Four Reasons I Came Back to Church." *Huffington Post*. April 2, 2012. Online: http://www.huffingtonpost.com/christian-piatt/four-reasons-i-came-back-to-church_b_1381025.html.

Powell, Mark Allan. *Loving Jesus*. Minneapolis: Fortress, 2004.

Quell, Gottfried, and Ethelbert Stauffer. "*Agapaō*." In *Theological Dictionary of the New Testament*, edited by Gerhard Kittel, translated by Geoffrey W. Bromiley. 1:21–55. Grand Rapids: Eerdmans, 1964.

Rohr, Richard. *Falling Upward: A Spirituality for the Two Halves of Life*. San Francisco: Jossey-Bass, 2011.

Smith, Gordon T. "The New Conversion: Why We 'Become Christians' Differently Today." *Christianity Today*. April 18, 2012. Excerpted from "Conversion and Redemption." In *The Oxford Handbook of Evangelical Theology*, edited by Gerald McDermott, 209–13 and 219–20. New York: Oxford University Press, 2011. Online: http://www.christianitytoday.com/ct/2012/aprilweb-only/new-conversion.html.

Teague, D. P. "The Biblical Metanarrative." *Postmodern Preaching*. Online: http://www.postmodernpreaching.net/metanarrative.htm.

Bibliography

Theodore of Mopsuestia. "Commentary on the Lord's Prayer and on the Sacraments of Baptism and the Eucharist." In *Woodbridge Studies* vol. 6, edited and translated by Alphonse Mingana, 11–23. Cambridge: W. Heffer & Sons, 1933.

Tinder, Glenn. *The Political Meaning of Christianity: The Prophetic Stance; An Interpretation*. New York: HarperSanFrancisco, 1991.

Warren, Rick. *The Purpose-Driven Life: What on Earth Am I Here For?* Grand Rapids: Zondervan, 2007.

Williamson, G. I. *The Westminster Shorter Catechism: For Study Classes*, 2nd ed. Phillipsburg, NJ: P&R, 2003.

Willimon, William H. "Impractical Christianity: Why Salvation in Jesus Christ Is Better than a Practice." In *A Spiritual Life: Perspectives from Poets, Prophets, and Preachers*, edited by Allan Hugh Cole Jr., 223–30. Louisville: Westminster John Knox, 2011.

———. *Who Will Be Saved?* Nashville: Abingdon, 2008.

Wright, N. T. *How God Became King: The Forgotten Story of the Gospels*. New York: HarperOne, 2012.

———. *Simply Christian: Why Christianity Makes Sense*. San Francisco: HarperSanFrancisco, 2006.

www.ingramcontent.com/pod-product-compliance
Lightning Source LLC
Chambersburg PA
CBHW070943160426
43193CB00011B/1788